PASCAL BOUQUILLARD

EDEN
THE FINAL SOLUTION

D1714664

To Pascale, my beloved

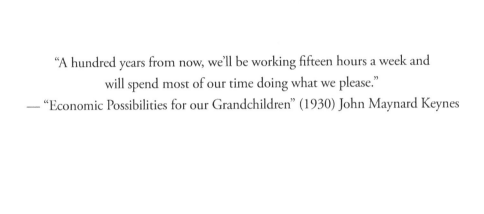

"A hundred years from now, we'll be working fifteen hours a week and will spend most of our time doing what we please."
— "Economic Possibilities for our Grandchildren" (1930) John Maynard Keynes

CONTENTS

FLASH FORWARD   1

EARTH   5

EDEN   151

FLASH BACK   257

GENESIS   261

FLASH FORWARD

JULY 4029

One of AGORAPP's weekly plenary lectures.
Today's agenda is the reproduction of Homo convertibilis
Translated from Edenian, the official language since 3877

Today's expert is Professor Rajesh Roah, *reintroduced* over forty times since his first cloning. He's going to talk to us about a major archaeological discovery that touches on the genesis of Edenian civilization:

"First of all, let me take a more general look at the Pierre de Vent for those of you who are only familiar with the part that governs our political system today. The origin of the name of this collection of fundamental and sacred texts comes from an inscription in French, engraved on the walls of the many cupolas that collapsed across Europe after the fall of the Cartels. French, may I remind you, was the language of communication between Edenians in some parts of Europe. The graphic study carried out by archaeologists has confirmed that the same instrument was used for this inscription as for all the engravings found on the remains of the domes protecting our ancestors from the great desertification. This collection brings together all the texts engraved by the man we have come to call "the founding father." It is because the material used to build these domes was non-biodegradable that we are fortunate enough to be able to analyze these texts of inestimable historical content. It should enable us to determine what belongs to our past and what is part of the myth. Analysis and comparison of bones found at numerous archaeological sites across the Western Hemisphere, in urban areas and under the ruins of domes, using the geographical coordinates revealed by the Pierre de Vent, has shown that some Edenians were accustomed to living in society and even had the ability to breed. The bones, of heterogeneous sizes and densities, demonstrate that a fatal incident probably interrupted the physiological cycle of the subjects studied, at different stages of their development. This extraordinary discovery has led researchers to

2

consider the possibility of a constant evolution of the individuals that formed the early Edenian species, Homo sapiens. This hypothesis runs counter to the fundamental principle of transplanting consciousness from one synthetic body to another — "the reintroduction"—which governs our way of life today, but which unfortunately also prohibits any population growth. For now, we are unable to determine at what point in its evolution Homo convertibilis lost the ability to multiply if it ever did. However, the theory on which most scientists agree is that Homo convertibilis supplanted Homo sapiens over an extremely short period of time, and after particularly violent confrontations. These confrontations took place almost everywhere on the planet, although in Africa the consequences were the most devastating, culminating in the almost total eradication of the continent. Unfortunately, the reasons and history of these conflicts have been lost in the ruins of the past. In addition, many reintroduction errors have taken place since the introduction of the first African specimens over two thousand years ago. We can only rely on the study of the Pierre de Vent to understand where we are coming from, in the hope of solving the mystery of creating life. Please find enclosed the most recent version of the founding fathers' Pierre de Vent, including the latest transcriptions reconstructed by the ecumenical commission. I invite you to continue reading on page 123, first verse."

EARTH

2054 – 2084

"Welcome to the society of great social advances, safety and progress."

Nucleus Orson

2054:
Extract from the *Pierre de Vent*,
Page 123, First Verse

"I don't see anyone, and as far as my memory goes, I can't remember any real contact. The only people I talk to are delivery people, when they bring me just about anything I could possibly want, from a simple pizza to the most sophisticated electronic equipment. Our interactions, when essential or when a signature is required, do not exceed forty seconds and fifteen words, most of the time always the same. What's more, their protective suits cover them completely, leaving only their eyes visible, which doesn't exactly facilitate communication. Finally, between answering machines managed by artificial intelligence and online services, direct contact, even at a distance, has become extremely rare. This is fine with me, because all too often, these contacts end in indictments. On more than one occasion, in general news documentaries broadcast on "Big Brother," my assisted multimedia device, I've seen sedentary people pay colossal fines, and even lose their sedentary status and their right to housing. This happened because they deliberately and repeatedly talked to a neighbor who ended up filing a complaint on online justice sites."

Raised in an incubator from anonymous donors, Winston was the product of the best combination that selected genes could compose. He was conceived in the hope of best meeting society's needs for major social advances, security and progress. Unfortunately, this reasoned and responsible demographic policy did not meet with unanimous approval. In other parts of the world, notably in the privatized territories of Africa, but also in Asia, populations continue to grow at rates that worry the governments of the three cartels. The most pessimistic estimates put the global population at over 12 billion, the vast majority of whom live below the legal poverty line. The authorities see this uncontrollable human proliferation as a potential danger to their hegemony, and a very real one for the future of the planet.

At the antipodes of these anarchic demographic developments, Winston pursues a rigorous and dispassionate education, provided by beings derived from industrial cloning, the SUBs. They have been the most effective solution to the problem of anthropophobia that has gradually poisoned social relations among the sedentary population, which Winston also suffers from. Each time they visit, they introduce themselves in the same way. "Hello, my name is 'SUB' and I'm going to have the pleasure of looking after you forever."

Winston quickly learned to recognize them, and none of them returned after his first four hours on the job.

Safe in his individual room, on appropriate educational sites, Winston soon realized that if he wanted to have fun, he first had to obey and learn. So he learned.

"I am unique and infinite; hell comes with the other." He has to repeat this at the start of each virtual session.

My neighbor, in the single room right next to mine, terrifies me. The sounds of his life limit my own existence. His presence is a threat, and I can only reduce it by barricading myself in my sedentary apprentice space. It's through the reassuring prism of my Big Brother control screen that I escape. He's the electronic window to the world that illuminates my existence. He's everything, which is probably why I've come to call my multimedia complex by this affectionate name. Unless it's one of the many expressions I hear during the shows I watch assiduously, I am not sure. That said, I don't watch just anything; I want to be able to choose! There are so many mind-numbing shows out there.

If the results of his MCQs are anything to go by, Winston will soon be useful to society. He hopes to obtain sedentary status by the end of the term. In fact, he has already been assigned a job when he finishes his studies. It will consist of gathering all data relating to the need for SUBs. In a region yet to be defined and for which he will be responsible, he will have to count their numbers and ensure that there is no lack of them anywhere.

"A colossal task, and essential for the smooth running of our progressive society," he has been told.

Outside, the industries of the 20th century have made the air unbreathable. This is one of the reasons behind their relocation to the privatized territories of Africa. Other reasons, it is claimed, are proximity to raw materials and cheap labor. Fortunately, inside the dwellings, the water is filtered and the staple food, the royal jelly, is distributed at will, saving the sedentary workers from starvation when the end of the month is too difficult to order anything else.

By the age of twelve, Winston had discovered solitary pleasures, stimulated by other appropriate sites. He patiently awaits the age when he can finally join the social networks that organize, in closed buses, expeditions sponsored by sperm banks. There he will participate in the gigantic harvest of gametes that civilization so badly needs to pursue research into improving SUB autonomy time.

For if the presence of others horrifies Winston, their bodies, on the other hand, are the ultimate object of his desires.

Winston fondly recalls the quote from "The New World" by Baptiste-Herbert Leonard, the old fallen philosopher:

"In these flask bodies, you'll distill your finest intoxication, and it's the indulgence of your desires that will shape the infinity of your individuality."

He lets his mind wander for a moment toward this coveted infinity. A shrill, singular notification from his multimedia complex forces him back into his immutable daily routine: it's time to log on to the account of the interactive site "OnlyFams" to meet his "Sugar Mummy." With a flick of his finger, he strokes the air and authorizes the connection. Jacqueline's hologram immediately lit up the kitchen area. In her sixties, she is the age Winston would want his mother to be if he'd had one. He'd imagined her small enough to be able to protect her, and almost peasant-looking, or at least as Winston imagined peasant-looking. Clean, but lacking in elegance and above all femininity, Jacqueline had been designed by the site to meet all Winston's expectations. She was literally his sugar mama, and the fact that she could only be a projection of artificial intelligence had long since ceased to worry him. "Good evening, my darling, have you remembered to take your portion of royal jelly? You know how important a balanced diet is for your health. I'm so worried when you don't do the right thing!"

"I'll do it right away, Mom," he answered meekly, as he would have liked to do as a child.

Winston opens the royal jelly tap, smiling tenderly at the hologram. He pulls out an edible paste that ripples gently down to the plate he always leaves there. This foodstuff already has the color and appearance, if not the smell, of what Winston's digestive system will transform it into after extracting its few rare nutrients. Like other sedentary people, he only decides to ingest this gastronomic aberration through subterfuge, such as his subscription to "OnlyFams."

What we wouldn't do to please our mother.

"That's fine, my darling," she says solemnly when everything is finished on the plate. "Now go brush your teeth and take your tetrahydrocannabinol; you know you need it to sleep."

Winston complies without question, before lying down on the bed, so conveniently installed right next to the kitchen. He soon begins to feel the effects of the cannabis derivative prescribed for all sedentary people and reimbursed by the social security system. As always, he is surprised by the opposite effects of this substance on the stiffness of his neck and the lightness of his head. He's never quite sure what happens next, but he's convinced he feels his sugar mom's hand slowly stroking his hair and whispering reassuring words. Words that only a real mom knows how to distill. It's 6:11 p.m. and, like every evening, Winston is fast asleep when the multimedia complex disconnects from "OnlyFams."

Report on sedentary apprentice
Pierre Banet

SUB #3927 completes his tour of duty and, as is the case at the end of every tour of duty, he modifies and completes the report drawn up by his predecessors. It is on this basis, and thanks to the brain recording of the previous clones responsible for Pierre, that he has been able to accomplish his task. He will be recycled at the end of his four-hour existence with the certainty of a duty accomplished.

"The results of the sedentary apprentice, Pierre Banet, continue to surprise both with their quality and their regularity. They have far exceeded anything that could have been expected from the combination of genes employed in his conception.

Lively, perceptive, analytical and cool, his mind is perfectly capable of taking the initiative when it's needed, without manifesting any desire for emancipation.

'He reached the end of his education but was never affected by the slightest sense of morality in any of the simulations to which he was subjected. He never hesitated to sacrifice what was necessary to carry out his missions. His decisions have always been pragmatic and directly linked to the goals set for him.

All simulations were successful.

Of a robust and attractive complexion, he is also capable of using seduction to achieve his ends but has so far shown no sincere sign of affection or recognition. A good knowledge of his perverse and violent tendencies will enable those in charge of him to better control his behavior and aspirations.

'Naturally dexterous and skilled, he'll have no trouble learning to handle weapons. So I recommend this apprentice for functions that go beyond the simple tasks usually assigned to sedentary people. I envisage for him a more decisive role, such as an officer in one of the private armies in Africa or in the delivery troops of one of the Cartel megacities."

March 1, 2059:
Excerpt from a news broadcast
on one of the world's countless channels
(in simultaneous translation)

African Green Clean has just lost its appeal and will have to be dissolved in the coming months. A fine of 150,000,000 WVU will have to be paid to the European government in damages. The scandal surrounding the government subsidies used to finance tests on the use of water hyacinth as a pollution control has now concluded. Several convictions have been made within the African company, and there is already talk of forthcoming indictments of high-ranking European officials. I would remind you that the company's CEO had managed to convince the European government that the new strain of Pontederia crassipes, developed in the laboratories of the privatized Congo, could depollute the rural desert and eventually allow the reintroduction of open-air crops. Everyone remembers the ecological catastrophe that followed, which led to the extinction of most of the country's major freshwater fish species. This judgment was handed down at a time when the experiment was about to be extended across Europe, particularly in France and Belgium. The first crops and the sites where the seeds were stored had to be incinerated to avoid any risk of invasion.

Awareness message from the Ministry of Welfare:

If, like many of us, you're a responsible and committed sedentary person, join our ranks by taking part in the "Sperm Bank" bus evenings. Through your donations, you can help the "Homo convertibilis" association in its research into cloning. This will ultimately increase the autonomy of SUBs tenfold, thus reducing transport and recycling costs. Your contribution is tax-deductible.

"To finish on a lighter note, I'd like to thank you for joining me on stage to welcome the beautiful Serena. Her new album, *Happiness in Capsules*, produced by the indefatigable Justin B. is being released on the Planet."

"Serena, why this title? A new fight?"

"Well, yes, I know how much people have suffered since the great dietary changes of recent decades: online medical services are overwhelmed with people who are depressed, suicidal or anemic. I want to tell them, through this album, that this great misfortune is not inevitable. Laboratories have developed an incredible new treatment that can restore vitality and tone. The drug, called 'Jouvence,' has been approved by the 'Transparency Commission of the Health Authority' and is already on the market. So there's new hope for us all.

"At the end of the day, between suffering and living normally thanks to a single capsule, there is not much to debate!

"So, like me and a multitude to come, make the right choice. Don't let yourself be swayed by the skeptics, the conservatives, the anti-globalists—and there are fewer and fewer of them. Take this incredible remedy today and give yourself a new lease on life!"

"So it's a committed album?"

"Absolutely. Unhappiness is not inevitable when happiness is in the capsule."

"Thank you, Serena. This part of the news has been brought to you by Orson and Orson Laboratories. Enjoy your evening."

Winston barely has the strength to mute Big Brother. He needs some silence to think. Even though he deeply dislikes silence, his lack of energy forbids any simultaneous activity, and he has to make a decision.

Should he believe all those conspiracy theorists, those pessimists who blame the new food order for his increasingly insurmountable fatigue and spend his entire salary on overpriced alternative foods about which he hears so much controversy? Or should he invest in these new miracle capsules that slow down aging and will, according to Serena, give him back some of his former energy? He has a deep admiration for Serena. The chronic exhaustion he has suffered from for so long has finally been acknowledged. He feels drained of all energy; now he realizes it, and he's not alone in having to overcome this state of exhaustion day after day, the cause of which he doesn't know.

"If it's not the diet that's responsible for my chronic fatigue," he says to himself, "what is it? When I think about it, I've got the best society has to offer: I've had an excellent education. I've got a respectable job and a humble but comfortable life. No health worries, and if I did, free online medicine assisted by Artificial Intelligence is at my disposal, with no waiting and no charge. No violence, and in the event of conflict between sedentary people, free online justice delivers its verdict in an instant. Of course, I've never used these services, but the advertisements are quite clear on the subject. 'My safety is the number one concern of all Cartel leaders'."

Winston has never found himself in a dangerous situation. The company's new organization is exemplary in this respect. Working from home and virtual conferences have put an end to all business travel, resulting in considerable time savings for the sedentary and the almost immediate disappearance of all forms of attack. The organization of nations within a cartel has made international conflict impossible, and although Winston is ultimately distressed to learn that in Africa, internal wars are decimating populations, he has no real worries at all.

Could he get tired of being too happy?

What does he need that he hasn't heard of?

Too many questions remain unanswered, and Winston has no one to turn to.

"I only have Serena, I have to trust her and do what she advises," he finally convinces himself. He often has tears in his eyes when he thinks so hard about her.

Winston had almost always known about working from home, an inevitable measure, he'd been taught at school, to combat galloping pollution and megalopolis congestion. He understood and lived with it, but it did limit his sources of information. As for the family, in the space of two generations, the law regarding public education had shattered what remained of it, and more and more births were to anonymous parents to suit society's needs.

This was his case.

To learn more about the cure, he turns on Big Brother again and breaks the deafening silence of his apartment.

"Jouvence, treatment," he says as articulately as possible.

It's essential to question the legitimacy of information by checking it against other sources, he recites in his head as he did when he was younger at boarding school, on the virtual advice of educational websites.

Immediately, a sponsored link appears, confirming what he's already secretly been hoping for: his emotions are at their peak, as he meets Serena's angelic gaze and tempting body on the screen. Beneath this bewitching image, the words "Jouvence from Orson and Orson" introduce a slogan:

"Like Serena, increase your power tenfold and adopt the capsules of Jouvence."

(This product is highly carcinogenic; please consult the site of the Minister of Welfare).

"I don't have to hesitate. The decision's a no-brainer!"

The information converges, and Serena dispels any lingering doubts in Winston's mind. What's more, this product is almost free, much cheaper than alternative food.

Even on a sedentary salary like mine, it's possible. If the effects live up to expectations, the whole planet will be snapping it up, so I've got to act fast, he thought.

In three clicks, he realizes that the stocks offered on the web are already sold out. However, it is still possible to obtain samples from itinerant retailers for those who have not yet reached their outdoor quota.

Going out?

How long has it been since I've been out? Winston had no idea. He remembers the dates of the first travel-reduction law he learned in seclusion classes, "to limit the emission of greenhouse gases." He was a young, sedentary apprentice when the law encouraging and then forcing people to work from home was passed. Finally, the law banning all individual travel had put an end to the last outdoor activities.

This was to limit the expense of treating illnesses caused by pollution and exposure to the sun's rays, which have become fatal.

The street is silent and deserted. Not a soul. Since the Solidarity Acts, the homeless have been systematically taken in and placed in rehabilitation centers. There, they receive the necessary vocational training and can then productively reintegrate into a society that cares for all its members with great concern for equality and justice. Sedentary people like Winston, on the other hand, live, work and play at home, thanks to the Internet, downloads and home deliveries.

He remembers his history lessons, recounting the chronic congestion of public transport that claimed so many victims in the cities. He also remembers the extraordinary social advance that was the life wage for all sedentary people. Nor does he forget the laws on the right to housing that enabled him to live with dignity.

Getting out of the house is also legislated and limited to twice a year. Winston hasn't been out for so long that he's in no way jeopardizing his sedentary status, which he wouldn't want to do for anything in the world.

Outside, protected only by his mask, Winston is sweating, yet it's not hot. His heart beats almost as fast as when he's pedaling his indoor bike. Another puff of heat. Winston is scared for the first time. He'd already been a little apprehensive about graduating and getting his first job, but the success rates were so high that the worry was almost futile. So, he moves forward with the extreme caution of a delivery worker back in the days when the homeless were still on the streets.

At a street corner, Winston hears the characteristic sounds of a perpetual motion engine that he's seen so often on the news. He rushes over as much as he can, looking in all directions for danger, and discovers a truck stopped in the middle of the road. In the back, several people dressed in white seem to be addressing an impressive crowd of silent, motionless individuals.

"I'm not the only one who's had the idea of going out, am I?" says the naive man with great concern.

The lab assistants' speeches are incomprehensible from this distance, and Winston decides to get closer. On the side of the truck, Winston reads, "Orson and Orson."

No one dares look at anyone, and prospective customers prefer to keep their eyes glued to the demonstrators rather than meet their neighbors.

Winston, like all the others, has always hated crowds. The presence of others immediately makes him uncomfortable. Nevertheless, driven by the desire to know more about Jouvence and the secret hope of obtaining a capsule or two, Winston resolves to step between the human skittles. They unilaterally separated themselves by the regulation of two meters, without anyone having asked or checked. The human geometric figure immediately adjusts nervously to this new parameter in order to continue to respect an unspoken rule that nobody seems to want to break.

Winston is not surprised, however, by the resemblance of their ridiculous configuration to the bowling game that all sedentary people have on their Multimedia Complex, especially as they all wear white clothes. How could he be surprised, since it goes without saying for a sedentary person to dress in what the status of a sedentary person makes available to him? This nurse's outfit is one of them. Of course, the state doesn't force anyone to dress in this way. Gradually, everyone has succumbed to the temptation of settling for the basic uniform, prioritizing savings to fund the things they believe they lack in order to make their lives complete.

Winston listens religiously to all the contraindications recited by the demonstrators, even though he already knows them. He also agrees to listen again to Serena's interview on the giant screen on top of the truck. His foot hurts, but he says nothing, asks no questions, and could have waited a long time without complaining when the representatives decided to start distributing the miracle drug. To tell the truth, everyone is delighted. No one moves for a long time after the distribution has stopped, like those dogs from a bygone era who used to stare at you intently after getting a treat in the hope of getting another.

Winston is able to purchase three capsules. He is delighted and places them under the high protection of his hands in each of his pockets. He's ready to turn back and return to the reassuring coldness of his stale little interior when he suddenly notices something out of the corner of his eye that seems most suspicious. A group of people who don't respect any safety distance are walking toward him with determined steps. No doubt about it, it must be a group of homeless, those vile beings who reject the system and prefer to confront pollution and shame rather than their responsibilities. He loathes these people in secret. He doesn't understand them and is therefore very afraid of them, even though most of them are extremely thin and ill from malnutrition.

Winston presses on and realizes with apprehension that the group is doing the same. He's now convinced they're after his precious treasure.

Winston changes his course and takes the side streets, trying to lose them at the risk of losing himself. He's running now, despite his fatigue, his many aches and pains and the weakness of his heart, which is beating in his chest to the point of breaking his ribs. He turns his head to check the distance separating him from his would-be torturers and loses his balance. Refusing to take his hands out of his pockets, he sprawls out, seriously scratching his face and knees in the process. He lies there, motionless and pitiful, unable to get up and resume his escape.

"I'm screwed!" he articulates mechanically, letting the air escaping from his mouth play with the puddle of liquid in which he has involuntarily rested his head.

2059:
Elsewhere, investors foundation meeting

"My friends, the promotion of our latest Jouvence product is a real success. All stocks, even those on the roadshows, have been sold out."

Nucleus Orson is delighted. Delighted by his business genius and his exceptional success, delighted to be able to show it all off again before the conquered assembly of members of the Investors Foundation of which he had become president. However, he did not create this foundation. Over a hundred and fifty years ago, in other parts of the world, other geniuses before him—Rhodes, Milner or Bilderberg—had imagined and developed a new form of power, on the bangs of government.

The principle is simple and profoundly judicious—Remain in the shadow of the puppet governments of every country and political party they control. It's essential to have a firm grip on all parties, regardless of ideology, in every country they control, to avoid being slowed down by unexpected political changes. This is extremely costly, but anything is possible when you consider that the Foundation alone holds more than two thirds of the world's wealth.

It's also essential that all the countries under their control are governed by the unifying principles of representative democracy and elections. In this way, power-hungry political puppets are at the mercy of their voters. To get re-elected by the sedentary masses, you need a lot of money. You have to communicate, imagine and present your program. Defend your convictions, even if they are opportunistic and costly. The necessary money is therefore kindly made available to the parties by the Investors Foundation, which quickly becomes essential to them.

Essential? The game is up: the president of this highly selective Foundation can now impose his laws, be above the law and become the law.

By 1912, the previous members of the Foundation already had control of the media and education. They were thus able both to direct political opinion and to select and groom future Foundation members. There is no racism or nationalism in this Foundation, only intelligence, achievement and community of interest.

Since that time, and thanks to Nucleus, the Foundation has further expanded its influence and greatly improved its revenues: The Foundation also lends substantial funds to countries around the globe, via private banks owned by its members. These virtual funds are merely numbers added to or transferred from one account to another. However, they generate very real interest that can end up ruining creditor countries engaged in the race for growth. Above all, they enrich the lenders. Thus, in less than two centuries, the Foundation has come to control education, the media, politics and the global economy in complete anonymity. The "Investor Foundation" has reached such a level of success that there is no more wealth or power to conquer; it owns it all.

And Nucleus is its president.

2059

In the half-light of his small, standard interior, Winston stands as rigid, lanky, and inexpressive as ever. Hope, however, keeps him wide awake, despite the new aches and pains that remain after his fall. He was wrong; no one was after his new acquisition. He ran away for nothing, and the homeless barely exchanged a few mocking smiles as they passed him, half-drowned in his puddle.

However, not even the memory of this humiliation can overcome the sudden euphoria that grips him. He would like to test the effects of this miracle product immediately, but the dosage is categorical: never take more than one tablet a day and never in the evening, at the risk of suffering serious side effects. After fear, it's excitement that gradually takes hold of him. Another emotion that until now had never reached such intensity. He's no longer sweating, but as before, his heart is beating faster and harder. He hears it in his ears, resonating like the African drums of one of Serena's songs, and he's happy.

Yes, he feels happy. There's no doubt about it, those shivers that run down his back and warm the top of his skull and his ears are shivers of happiness. For the first time, he hopes, almost dreams. Suddenly he thinks of the risks and side effects.

"Jouvence side effects," he says, breaking the sickly silence of his apartment.

Big Brother immediately performs the requested search and within fractions of a second, Winston discovers them on his wall screen:
Common:

- Tachycardia, Arrhythmia
  - Dizziness
  - Mood disorders
  - Headaches
  - Insomnia, agitation

20

Undefined frequency:

- Coma
- Myocardial infarction
- Respiratory failure
- Increased libido, hypersexuality.
- Persistent genital arousal syndrome/prolonged erections

Winston's eyes glide nonchalantly over the first descriptions: it's been a long time since all those warnings caught the attention of sedentary people: tobacco and alcohol kill, food poisons and ointments are carcinogenic, and yet everyone uses them.

On the other hand, he has never read anything like the last two warnings:

- Persistent genital arousal syndrome and prolonged erections.

What an unusual side effect! He thinks.

It has to be said that since the disappearance of the family unit and philosophers, as well as the gradual but irremediable disaffection of the world's religions, morality is no more than a vague memory. Sex, on the other hand, is everywhere. In the media and in the daily lives of those who still find the necessary energy within themselves. Winston lost his libido a long time ago, but the prospect of regaining it is not without displeasure.

Maybe I'll be able to go back to the sperm bank bus parties with this thing, he thinks with a touch of mischief.

These buses, theaters of nights of unbridled lust, pick up amateurs at their homes so that they don't have to go outside and breathe the stale air. The service is free of charge, with just one condition: oocytes must be collected before entry, seeds must be collected with each ejaculation, and the precious flasks must be left behind when getting off the bus. The seed samples are then stored and made available to laboratories that will create new clones and continue their research on "Homo convertibilis," the SUB.

One of the advantages of these seed collections is that they are tax-deductible and offer sedentary "farmers" a very pleasant way of boosting their humble income.

Winston enjoyed it a few times, but soon his anemic body didn't have the strength, and he was forced to give it up. These few lustful thoughts soon overcame his last misgivings. He feverishly grabs the capsule of a thousand promises and swallows it without even taking the time to pour himself a drink.

Almost instantly, Winston experiences new sensations. Perhaps it's the power of suggestion? Whatever it is, he's never felt so alive. After a few hours of hoping, a glance in the mirror verifies this. No more dark circles under his eyes. His gaze is brighter and more sustained. While this gives him some hope, the rest of his body, on the other hand, gives him grief: Winston isn't tall, 5' 5" on his best days, but his lean frame gives him a slim appearance. He stands tall despite a lifetime of bending his back; no doubt a genetic reminder of a grandeur long forgotten.

"The time it took me to complete my training seemed interminable," says Pierre, stroking the DNA key in his pocket that the administration has just configured for him.

This key, connected to the vehicle assigned to it, creates a unique link between it and the machine that cannot be copied or misappropriated. If this link were to be broken, it would be simpler for the administration to destroy the vehicle rather than reprogram it. He has become a technological extension of Pierre. If a mission comes up, all he has to do is think of the destination and the vehicle will meet him where he is and take him there.

"I would never have imagined that I would have to spend so much time before becoming operational," he says.

Thought-control required months of training. Then there was the high-protection suit for deliveries, combat techniques to survive attacks by groups of homeless people, the principles of defusing explosives in the event of an "Ubuntu" terrorist attack, the handling of self-defense weapons and, of course, the various safety procedures relating to each type of delivery

"*Safety is the first freedom*," he was constantly reminded during his many internships.

"The delivery driver's job is undoubtedly one of the most difficult jobs this society has to offer," he muses, as he heads for his first real assignment as a job holder. "Difficult, but exciting," he adds, smiling broadly as his car approaches.

The door opens and he's ecstatic. In fact, no other civilian job offers such an opportunity to get out of his apartments and move around freely, or almost. He can also take the initiative, as his schedule is flexible and varied. Every day is an adventure of sorts, and the best part is that the monthly delivery person's bonus, on top of the lifetime salary associated with his sedentary status, is considerable. He smiles, because he would have been prepared to do this job for no pay at all.

A privileged member of the sedentary elite.

Pierre blushed with pleasure at the thought. He'd always known he was destined for an extraordinary future. Maybe he was even going to become one of those stars of the Multimedia complexes he's so fond of, a politician or a late night host, why not?

He turns on his monitor screen to his favorite program, the news, chasing his dream:

"The last queen bee and her few worker bees died this morning in Illinois, United States. Centuries of collaboration with mankind have come to an end. Since the end of the 20th century, the number of bees had declined dangerously. After numerous lawsuits and dismissals, researchers were never able to isolate the disease and put a lasting stop to the process. They are now an officially extinct species. This could have had disastrous consequences for our survival, were it not for the extraordinary and benevolent work of the "Otnesom" food company. It is offering and sponsoring this part of the news today.

"With Otnesom, no more allergies because nature becomes clean, and plants produce without pollen. With Otnesom, our food reserves are well guarded, and we breathe noticeably easier.

Otnesom also funds research into "GMO sperm and oocytes" resistant to pesticides in food.

On the other hand, promising news, the cloned cow DX504 is now in its sixty-fifth day of existence, which is considered very encouraging by scientists. Indeed, if DX504 passes the edibility tests and no signs of degeneration appear, this would be a decisive step toward the gradual restoration of edible meats that have disappeared since the second mad cow epidemic, which claimed millions of cartel victims and forced agricultural agents in producing countries to slaughter their entire herds of sheep, cattle, pigs and horses. International markets have already estimated the price of the first steaks at over 2,000 WVU (World Value Units) per kilo.

His delivery today is addressed to an "Electra J. Orson." She lives in a neighborhood he has never heard of. The SUB on duty even told him he wouldn't have to put on his protective delivery suit, as the air was breathable, and a dome protected the residence from the sun's rays. He can't wait to see it.

The streets are, of course, deserted and, for that very reason, poorly maintained, but the new "Perpetuity" vehicles provided for delivery drivers barely skim the ground, which considerably reduces the number of bumps caused by the uneven road surface.

"I'm flying!" he says to himself. "Luckily, this option is not available on this model; otherwise I would have been immediately propelled to cloud nine," he continues, congratulating himself on his irresistible sense of humor.

After a few minutes of intense self-satisfaction, Pierre's mind wandered through the chaotic geometry of streets and buildings until an incongruous movement in one of the perpendicular streets caught his attention. The car immediately slows down, then stops. The presumed activity is rather far down the street, but the sickly stillness of the rest of the scenery only accentuates any marginal activity. The glove compartment opens and offers Pierre the pair of binoculars he needs.

Two homeless people.

"Just my luck… I don't think they saw me."

The window opens softly, without the slightest sound, and without him having to do anything. Slowly, he takes out of his holster the proton rifle he's been entrusted with, which he's been dying to use.

Decidedly, they saw nothing and continued in the opposite direction to Pierre, but so slowly that he wasn't about to lose sight of them. In any case, he knows from his training that once the target is locked, there's no risk of a miss, even for a novice.

Pierre closes his eyes, not out of apprehension of the consequences of his gesture, but rather to enjoy it even more. Indeed, one of the silhouettes collapses without a sound to betray the action. Pierre is delighted; it's the smaller one that sinks, as it was harder to reach, and he's all the prouder for it.

Curiously, the other figure doesn't run away. It's a peculiar attitude that arouses the hunter's curiosity. He feels safe enough to take a closer look. He moves forward at a steady pace, but the distance is quite considerable. The surviving homeless person should have fled long ago. He would have had the time, even if this escape had not changed the fatal outcome Pierre has in store for him. He is now close enough to make out the faces. The victim must be eight or nine years old at most.

"The homeless are monsters to leave children that age on the streets!"

The other, a dirty, smelly female, is washing her cheeks with tears. She bends over the little body, reddened and fatally bruised. She takes a long moment before considering Pierre's presence and turning her head toward him.

"Should I rape her?" he says to himself, but immediately changes his mind, as the smell she gives off is simply unbearable. Without taking aim, he fires a point-blank salvo that rips off the woman's face and throws her body a few meters away from the other.

"I wonder what could possibly have linked these two pitiful beings," wonders Pierre as his vehicle approaches.

After several hours at a steady speed, the "Perpetuity" finally slowed down. For several kilometers now, Pierre can admire the protective vault above the neighborhood the clone had told him about.

He is extremely impressed.

Even more so when he enters the residence and discovers, for the first time, what until now only his history classes had mentioned: vegetation.

He has crossed a new threshold in his rise to fame. He suddenly senses that this is where his chances of success lie.

"Pierre, I must confess I'm very impressed by your tenacity and opportunism," exclaims Nucleus, president of the investors' foundation, offering his interlocutor a smile he usually reserves only for those he intends to ruin.

"Coming for a simple delivery and ending up in my office is certainly not an everyday occurrence."

As he finishes his sentence, Nucleus beckons Pierre to sit down. Pierre immediately realizes that this position will put him at a disadvantage if Nucleus remains standing, but he has no choice but to accept his invitation.

"I have, of course, made some inquiries about you following your request for an audience and once again, reading the many reports made by those who have been responsible for your education, I am very pleasantly surprised. So I'll get straight to the point, young man. Yes, I might have a position for you."

Pierre hadn't asked for anything yet; in fact, he hadn't even opened his mouth.

Without waiting for any reaction from Pierre, Nucleus continued, "Pierre, you're nothing, even less than nothing: you're a sedentary. Your existence is only as interesting and meaningful as I want it to be."

Pierre is outraged, but immediately understands that this is only a prelude, an introduction. The man in front of him is so powerful, he exudes such a sense of grandeur that there can be no real contest between them. Pierre doesn't stand a chance, he knows it, and all his past successes vanish into the void of this overwhelming realization.

"You see, I'm interested in you. Yes, absolutely, and I'll tell you why. All I have around me are people of great wealth, but many of them are incapable of helping me, far too busy making money for themselves. I can't share with them any of my intentions or any of my projects. I'm hopelessly alone. I'm alone and

27

you're nothing, so there's a way to do business here, don't you think? I offer you to become my assistant, and you, in return, offer me your existence."

Pierre can't believe it, doesn't know what to say or even what to think. He is literally petrified. Is this the chance of a lifetime, or the day of his death?

Nucleus doesn't care about Pierre's silence and concludes, "In a way, my dear delivery boy, either you manage to convince me of your complete and unalterable loyalty, or your pitiful and useless life ends here, right now. I must admit, you have very little room for maneuvering," adds Nucleus in a joking tone that only he can perceive.

Pierre still hasn't said anything.

"Incidentally, I've got a first field assignment for you with a certain Catherine, who will show me what you're capable of. She's far less quick witted than you, but asks far too many questions if I'm to believe the artificial intelligence reports on the electronic archives of her Internet searches and personal documents. If all goes well, I'll let you meet regularly with some of your peers on my behalf, assess the situation and make the appropriate decision. After that, I'll take the time to explain to you the broad outlines of the global situation along with my aspirations and plans."

Before Nucleus had finished his sentence, he left the room, leaving Pierre alone to ponder what he might have said during this incredible interview.

Nucleus knows that cow DX504 will never die, because it doesn't exist. For decades, he and his fellows have been feasting on cloned steaks, made from meat produced in laboratories, at far too high a cost for a sedentary person to ever consider tasting it. One thing led to another, and Nucleus remembered a quotation he'd stumbled across while perusing a book on revolutions published in 2024. The author[i] quoted Edward Levingston Yumans, a champion of Social Darwinism, in the 19th century. His theory defended the idea that people should be subject to the same laws of evolution as plants and animals.

Asked what solutions he envisaged to society's problems, he replied, "Absolutely nothing; it's all a question of evolution. Maybe in four or five thousand years, evolution will have taken mankind beyond its present limits, but for the moment, there's nothing we can do about it."

This extraordinary theory had completely overturned Nucleus' vision of the world. *Laissez-faire*, taken to the extreme and scientifically justified. Natural selection at its most advanced. The individual is no longer a creature in the image of the divine, with a unique and priceless soul; he is the fruit of general evolution, and we have to accept that some beings are more resistant, surviving and multiplying while others succumb and disappear. Since that day, Nucleus had become a champion of Social Darwinism. Better still, he has made a point of proving these theories by demonstrating that, even in the context of total welfare, the weakest will perish anyway.

For this reason, Nucleus became the architect and promoter of the extraordinary social advances of his time: lifelong wages, company housing and unlimited distribution of royal jelly, the staple food of the sedentary population.

Unfortunately, even if he's convinced he's right, the experiment lasts too long and the planet's imbalance accelerates. He is even one of the privileged few who really know how bad things are, since his group controls the media. On the screens of the sedentary, there is little information on the subject, and when it becomes inevitable, the bad news is drowned in a flood of contradictory information that makes it lose all credibility. Yet the reality is simple and inescapable. The earth is parched, devitalized, its oceans moribund and its atmosphere far too rich to breathe. Unchecked population growth has exceeded the most alarming forecasts made at the start of the century, and the earth's population is approaching twelve billion. The vast majority of this population is poor, ignorant and barely surviving. Nucleus even added to this grim description at his Foundation's last general meeting:

"Poor, ignorant and useless."

Indeed, the new economic principles, based on fictitious speculation and interest rates, allow the richest to enrich themselves without having to produce, sell or even promote their services to the greatest number. In the race for growth, it's the interest on money that makes money. Wealth has become esoteric, multiplying in the accounts of those who already have so much they don't know what to do with it. At present, the "futureless," as Nucleus calls those who have to rent out their time to producers or governments, are not only useless to the economy, but harmful to the planet: not enough food, not enough water, not enough air or space.

Over and above the social advances introduced by Nucleus, certain achievements such as medicine cannot be completely called into question without risking an awakening of the conscience of sedentary populations, which Nucleus wants to avoid at all costs. By treating the sick, social Darwinism and natural selection can't work as quickly as he'd like, and planetary equilibrium is jeopardized. At one point, the Nucleus group tried to discredit vaccines, hoping to let as many people as possible die, but only the oldest perished, which didn't help their cause.

However, there's no question of his little paradise being jeopardized by a trivial problem of stewardship, and Nucleus has a plan that will revolutionize the medical field.

The first part of this revolution is called Jouvence.

A few days later

Since first taking Jouvence, Winston has left his room every night to go to the bus and experience hallucinatory moments of intensity that have nothing in common with his first experiences of state-sponsored debauchery; those before the medication.

After a hard day's work, Winston prepares for a wild evening out. This new routine has become almost as enjoyable as the evening itself. Winston is discovering what others before him have learned to savor: "the delights of waiting." In just a few days, he's learned how to enjoy himself, when until now he'd barely been able to survive.

His looks are unrecognizable: he has completely shaved his body and conscientiously maintains it every day. He spends almost his entire sedentary salary ordering his Jouvence capsules, beauty treatments, moisturizers. The downside is he needs to feed exclusively out of the royal jelly from the state sponsored intestinal transits. It has such a pasty texture and is so unappetizing when the home dispenser defecates it with metronomic regularity as soon as he presses the push button. But one has to make sacrifices.

"In the end, it's not as bad for your health as the conspiracy theorists say. These scumbags denigrate the efforts of our government and sap our morale," he rants to give himself courage every time he has to feed on it.

He even ordered a UV station on credit, which is starting to give surprising results. His whole being feels regenerated, despite his sad diet. But what never ceases to excite him is what his penis is now able to do. What used to be just a continuation of his bladder, enabling him to empty it with varying degrees of success, has now become his alpha and omega, the brush and the work of art, the instrument and the music. He lives for that alone. By sheer willpower, his limb can take on any size, any rigidity, for as long as he likes. Yesterday in agony, his power today seems limitless.

In the silence of the street, the bus purrs like a pussy in heat. Washed, shaved, taloned and perfumed, Winston closes the door of his apartment, determined to do even better than previous nights. His veins swollen with youth and his penis hard, he knows he's expected, and under no circumstances does he want to disappoint.

The door opens and time is suspended as the bus prepares to digest its night rations. The flesh is multicolored and the scents are rich and musky. To the music of thalassotherapy times, bodies enter in cadence. In this shared boudoir, names are ignored, tongues are tied and hands are lost. Winston slips out of his synthetic cocoon and, the sextant all risen, smears his oversized pistil across the offered canvas of his admirers.

Carried along by a warm current of vaginal fluid, he boldly penetrates his first conquest. She gives herself, arches her back, bends, tenses and surrenders. Winston places himself in these erotic hostilities like a piece of mortar on a battlefield: mobile, powerful and devastating. With one woman's breast in his hand, he licks without moderation the overflowing vulva of another, sitting on his face, overwhelmed with pleasure as yet another straddles him. He doesn't penetrate her; she impales herself on his member stretched to cloud nine. She cries out. Is it pain or pleasure? Winston doesn't care because he's besieged on all sides and not ready to give up even a tiny part of his treasure. On the contrary, he forages and pulls himself up. Everyone's perspiration makes it easier to change positions, and the most daring projections are thus facilitated.

Here he is, lost in the ass of the woman who was devouring her neighbor's penis with her O-shaped mouth. With a powerful, deep and steady movement, he wrings cries of pleasure from his partner of the moment, which thunders above the general hubbub of jerky moans, groans and whispered dirty promises. Winston may be competing for first place in the evening's stallion rankings, but the other males are fighting like hell. The main thing is that nothing gets lost. It doesn't matter if you ejaculate, if the next moment the member is erect again. If it's erect, she grabs it and places it wherever she pleases. All night long, the insatiable females cum to the point of insanity, and the males pour their semen into latex test tubes until they run dry.

Physical bliss, liberated from all mental control, when only instinct has a say, when the other is desired to the point of wanting to feed on him, only then does existence reclaim its rights. In this tide of sperm, sweat, saliva and intimate secretions, in this hormonal mire, the meaning of life is finally rediscovered. After all, isn't it in manure that the most beautiful plants grow?

In this desperate race, where each athlete refuses to forfeit, the only way to accompany the return of the sun is to get off at the bus stop when the bus arrives.

Only eight people will die tonight. They reveal themselves as the crowd of lovers gathers. The victims of love, as they are portrayed in the media, most often end up suffocated under their partners or simply overworked to the extreme, their hearts stop beating. Who wants to wait ninety-seven years to die?

Maybe tomorrow, they think softly as they leave the theater of their lovemaking, their bodies full and heavy, perfectly exhausted and emptied of substance in every sense of the word.

For everyone, it's almost time to get back to work, and even if it's a bit tedious, it's essential to the sedentary status they're so proud of. By the time Winston comes to his senses, the bus is long gone. His sex is aching, his body weary and bruised as in the worst moments of his pre-Jouvence life. A drug addict on the wane, it's time for him to take another capsule.

Every morning, Catherine sees Winston come in through the peephole. For years, the only evidence of her neighbor's existence was Serena's music. He sometimes listened to it to the point of bursting his eardrums. But for the past few months, she'd caught him going out several nights a week, looking as dapper as a young prime, and coming home every morning anemic and ill.

Catherine didn't buy anything of her education or of the great social advances. She only became sedentary by cunning to avoid becoming homeless, hiding her doubts and suspicions behind a clay complexion and faded blue eyes. She's only used her Big Brother since paper and pencils are no longer on sale online. She has, however, fitted herself with a virtual private network that ensures her total anonymity, guaranteed by the manual. Since then, reassured, she has transcribed her questions, her anxieties and her secret desire for revolution, which she can barely put into words because she's so afraid of it. All she does is write pages and pages of theories about the new social contract, rehabilitation centers, online public health and justice services, delivery person brutalities, and sperm bank buses she's vaguely heard of but distrusts. Even the source of the royal jelly, which Catherine eats daily, raises questions that terrify her: what are its real ingredients; is it the cause of her extreme fatigue? She doesn't listen to the official media, refuses advertising even to save a few WVU, meticulously selects political analysis sites after lengthy research on the "darknet," and entertains herself exclusively with a CD and DVD library of old 20th-century albums and films that nobody wants anymore and that she has delivered at great expense.

Her only concession to contemporary culture is Serena's album collection, which she discovered through the wall she shares with Winston and has become fond of. She also collects antediluvian CD/DVD players, which she has to buy at virtual flea markets and replace regularly, as there are no spare parts left for these devices from another age.

One morning, endowed with an excess of courage and her ear glued to her front door, Catherine dared to ask, "How was it?"

Winston, in his downward phase like every morning of debauchery, thinks he's hallucinating and stops dead in his tracks, waiting for another sentence to confirm the balance of his sanity.

Still trembling from her audacity, Catherine can't produce a sound, and a few minutes of silence later, overcome by fatigue, Winston resumes his journey to his lodgings.

When he finally reaches the door, Catherine has regained some of her composure. "How were the buses tonight?" she tries again.

Winston replies, "Excellent, thank you." Then he opens the door and collapses on his bed, covered by a few relics of his previous day's outfit.

The next day, during the workday, he remembers, like a bad dream, the high-pitched voice from nowhere and the short exchange that followed. He regularly opens his door to check that the person he thinks he spoke to isn't waiting on the landing for him to come out.

"I must be losing it", he whispers to himself before closing the door.

"No," suddenly answers the door on the landing opposite him.

Winston stops, eyes wide, completely stunned.

"Who's there?" he exclaims, torn between anger and fear.

"Catherine," replies Catherine, almost regretfully.

Winston approaches the door, driven by an unhealthy curiosity he didn't know he had, while hoping it won't open. Catherine obviously has no intention of opening it.

"Do you live here?" he asks stupidly. As if it could be otherwise!

"Yes," says Catherine, who doesn't think any harder than he does.

Since this unprecedented event in both their lives, Catherine and Winston have been talking regularly. Oh, of course, Catherine never opens the door, so they talk on either side of their proverbial booth, just as the Catholics used to do at confession back in the days of the great religious myths. At first, they had to learn to use their vocal cords in a sustained way, and they often ended their conversations voiceless, for lack of training, but little by little things fell into place. Once they'd finished exchanging all the platitudes that come with rediscovering social life, the questions became more precise, more pertinent and more personal. Soon enough, Winston convinces Catherine to meet him at a different time than just after his nocturnal jaunts.

"Precisely," she asks him that evening, "you are coming back from an evening on the bus. Aren't you?"

"Of course," replies Winston. "It's fun, you know, and it's useful to society; you should go!"

Catherine doesn't respond to this invitation. She is still afraid of being bugged, or expecting to find out the hard way that Winston is a government spy whose mission is to get her to comment negatively on this legal, non-profit-making activity so that she loses her status. She's well aware that such an eventuality is highly unlikely, but she doesn't want to take any chances.

Without waiting for an answer, Winston closes his door on the night.

In his European office, Malcolm O'Brien is part of one of the three ministries whose activity governs the work of every sedentary person on the planet. This position represents for him the culmination of a sedentary career spanning more than thirty years, and he imagined that at this professional level he would have a better idea of how work is organized in the Cartels. As it turns out, that is not the case.

In this job, as in previous ones, work has been so sectorized and automated that every day, on his computer desk, the work of the sedentary staff forms a virtual pile. He can't really understand its purpose or deduce its next steps. Pages and pages of text, tables and graphs commenting on surveys and research, justifying bills and analyzing budgets. The principles of the 20th century tertiary sector pushed to the extreme and crowned as the master's piece of the absurd.

If O'Brien had to print it all, he'd probably have had to leave the room. Yet this is only the output of a single day's work in one of the ministries' offices. Every day, he receives just as many. It would take a team of thirty people with solid knowledge in all fields to read all this. But his job is not to read these documents, but simply to file them, in alphabetical order by author's name, in folders shared with others hierarchically higher up than him. In fact, it's not even he who does the sorting—the computer does it for him. Nor is he responsible for the computer's maintenance, which depends on an external site with which he has never had any dealings, since everything is done remotely.

In a new surge of consciousness, O'Brien couldn't stop his mind from wondering how far up the hierarchy he has to go to make the work done by the sedentary staff meaningful. However, he knew that he must never go beyond the thought stage, without risking jeopardizing his own situation.

He sometimes regrets not having tried his luck in the privatized territories of Africa. It was to this continent that the entire consumable goods production industry was relocated, after many African countries were bought up by private sector industrialists to pay off the national debts of these bankrupt countries. Many employees followed this migration and went into exile to keep their jobs, not him.

I hear life there is very different.

"I'd never have had the guts to live there," he says to himself.

He knows that this continent is plagued by the twin problems of exponential overpopulation and the shrinking of non-privatized inhabitable areas and torn apart by appalling wars of independence that have turned Cartel factories into true fortresses. This situation makes it possible to sell off almost all the industrial world's weapons production and keep production costs at a derisory level but makes life impossible for expatriates.

One of the pillars of this private industry is the production of buses used by the sperm banks of the three cartels to harvest the gametes needed for SUB cloning research.

O'Brien recalls with a certain melancholy the beginnings of this very special donation system.

Initially, back in the days when open-air outings were regulated but not yet forbidden, the need for human seeds and oocytes required by the clonal industry had prompted sperm banks to innovate in the art of collecting samples. No longer able to rely on volunteers alone, they created a new kind of event.

Sedentary people wishing to forget their worries of the week met on Fridays and Saturdays in specially built "pleasure centers," where everything was organized so that social barriers and fear of the other dissipated for the evening. Admission was free for women participating in the egg harvest, but prohibitively expensive for men. However, once inside, alcohol and soft drugs were distributed at discretion, and the dance music was deafening and progressively hypnotizing. The half-light of suggestive cinematographic projections, the psychedelic lights and the stifling atmosphere of these confined spaces encouraged participants to abandon themselves, by choice or weakness, to the pleasures of the flesh. The organizers had come up with an ingenious and motivating system.

Men who took the trouble to collect the semen produced during their intercourse in the containers provided at the entrance had their entrance fee refunded. In other words, most of them managed to have their naughty evenings paid for.

O'Brien had lived through this transitional period. Then the "public health" law was passed, forbidding more than two outings a year due to the extreme risk of sun radiation exposure and pollution, and it became impossible to attend these parties. To compensate for this sudden and terrible drop in production and harvesting, the sperm banks, whose needs seemed to be growing all the time, had set up a system of buses to pick up participants as they left their homes (the vast majority of sedentary people live in apartments in huge multi-story blocks of flats) and to take them to the nearest center. Unfortunately, the pick-up was long and tedious, and users often started "partying" before the bus had finished its rounds. Bringing along makeshift sound systems and their own hallucinogens, users found a way to break the acute malaise caused by the interminable wait, combined with a degree of promiscuity made unbearable by their inactivity.

Gradually, the buses became wider, longer and equipped for anonymous egg harvesting. The gentle swaying caused by the slow, contemplative wanderings of this new-age public transport as it wandered through the streets deserted by decree, on routes calculated to ensure that everyone was home by daybreak, added to the sultry charm of these nocturnal meetings. The number of participants increased tenfold in just a few months.

As a result, the pleasure centers were closed and converted into rehabilitation centers for the homeless. Representatives from across the political spectrum agreed that this was an extraordinary step forward in the fight against social fracture and in favor of greater morality.

O'Brien knew all about these bus tours. He was still young then, and no one wasted the opportunity to spend nights "partying at the princess's expense."

Now, O'Brien has long since lost the age, inclination and strength to participate in these getaways, and retirement is just around the corner. He's dreading the change. He'll have to leave his company apartment and move into one of the retirement homes offered to him by the healthcare insurance company, only to discover, he dreads, a new form of boredom. In an attempt to chase away these bad thoughts, he decides to do something he has rarely done in his entire career:

open a file sent by one of the sedentary staff for whom he was, in theory, the superior. It was a study on new bus models.

The innovations are impressive, and these buses are unquestionably state-of-the-art.

Firstly, the widening of roads and the straightening of the main arteries along which the sedentary residents' homes were built allowed for the construction of buses as wide as the old, prefabricated, detached houses. Their length is just as impressive, and the report states that it is almost impossible to consider all users passing each other on the same evening.

With the advent of perpetual motion engines and the spread of artificial intelligence, it is no longer necessary to drive the vehicles, so the buses are, of course, driverless. But what seems to most inspire the author's admiration are the new sanitary facilities installed at each end of the vehicle and equipped with an almost instantaneous system for filtering and recycling dirty water. A prototype system which, if it proves effective, will be extended to the rehabilitation of some of the most polluted aquifers.

O'Brien stops reading, or perhaps it's his eyes that stop looking and can only see.

He is gradually coming to understand the true meaning of the social advances that everyone brags about.

His housing and retirement depend on his work. It's certainly not at his age that he's going to question the system and risk losing everything.

Professional activity is a precious right. It is the basis of everything. If you lose it, you lose your identity, your independence and your freedom.

O'Brien closes the file. All too often, the isolation in which he finds himself plunges him into deep confusion. He is in his house like a hamster in its cage. He can, if he wishes, spin the carpet of his treadmill to turn his desolation into perspiration, sit at his desk and even read the files and perhaps understand them, or switch on his multimedia screen and dream of the freedom of those artists who feed his meager entertainment.

They still seem to enjoy some kind of purpose in life. For his part, this purpose has long been alienated to him. He lives by reflex, to do as all those he never meets, but who form with him the great disunited family of the sedentary.

Nietzsche maintained that a sick person who ended his life almost deserved to live. Today, by calmly opening the window of his home, Malcolm O'Brien can finally justify his presence on earth.

After two days without any sign of him, the sedentary members of the higher hierarchy reported a malfunction in the chain of filing of administrative reports in the "cleaning and public hygiene" department. The intervention units of the European Democratic Government discovered his body smashed on the pavement that no sedentary people have bothered reporting. A few hours later, his position and apartment were assigned to another.

Catherine opened her door to Winston; almost without meaning to. Winston shared with her such overwhelming news that her hand decided to lower the door handle without warning her, in order to add to her words the physical weight of her protest.

A position has just become available in one of the three ministries that regulate the professional activities of the Cartel's sedentary population. He has just been offered the position of O'Brien.

This activity has absolutely nothing to do with his previous SUB training, but the message has assured him of a smooth upgrade and the certainty of a more comfortable salary. If he accepts, he will, of course, have to move into the residences reserved for senior civil servants. He'll have to leave.

Catherine is petrified. It's as if her heart just skipped two or three beats

As shaken as she was, standing on the stoop like a delivery person without his regulatory outfit, Winston smiled stupidly, interrupting a sentence that he barely remembered starting.

"Are you going to leave?" continues Catherine's mouth, complicit in her hand. Catherine blushes at the temerity of her question and vows to regain control of her senses and her body.

"No," he replies a little too quickly and a little too loudly, "because I'd have to stop going to bus parties, and I don't want to stop."

A wave of relief crashes over her, but there's something else there. Disappointment, perhaps, in Winston's lack of drive.

"Come on in."

On the kitchen table next to Catherine's bed, Winston spots a very unusual object. In the course of their encounter, he has come to know his neighbor's offbeat world, studded with anachronistic objects and conspiratorial thoughts.

He should worry about her, he should denounce her but denouncing her means losing her. Winston likes having her around. "He won't tell the authorities," he concludes, grabbing the unusual object to chase away his deviant thoughts.

"Do you know what it is?" asks Catherine, smiling, savoring his ignorance in anticipation.

"No!"

"It's a laser stylus. It's a traditional way of engraving inscriptions or drawings on all kinds of surfaces. Can you write calligraphy?"

"No."

Winston would have liked to answer something else, but the SUBs never taught him anything other than how to type on a keyboard. More often than not, he just dictates what he wants to write, so calligraphy, he's not even exactly sure what that means.

"Come on, I'll give it to you, I've got a case full of it. I'll give it to you on one condition: you let me teach you. It was considered art, you know?"

Winston doesn't give a damn about calligraphy, but he doesn't have the strength to contradict Catherine, and besides, *she'll get tired before he does* he thinks.

Winston finds Catherine rather ugly, which reassures him greatly. He has no desire to continue at home the activity he hones night after night on the sperm bank buses.

Catherine finds Winston smaller than the peephole suggests. It doesn't matter to her past mere observation; she's not attracted to men anyway.

As the visits progress, however, carried along by the intimacy of their conversations and the exhausting rigor of Catherine's calligraphy classes, their hands come to touch, their skins to cross. She finds his talent and facility, and he falls for it.

It's a perfectly pointless activity, he tells himself regularly. But contact with this device that digs out words on any surfaces at his whim gives him a sense of power and control he's never felt before. He wouldn't have missed his daily lesson for the world. Within a few months, she has nothing left to teach him and they simply take infinite pleasure in each other's words. In these moments, their hearts beat harder and often in unison. Sometimes, tears drown their eyes for a reason that escapes them. Some mornings, when Winston is late in coming home, Catherine feels a twinge in her heart and a weight on her chest. She has considered logging on to the online doctor for a consultation several times, despite the fact that they were the last people that she'd ever trust. Curiously, all symptoms immediately dissipated at the precise moment she heard Winston's footsteps on the stairs. Winston, for his part, often thinks of Catherine and fears for her safety.

All those absurd conspiracy theories she's been filling the pages of her Big Brother with are likely to get her into trouble. What will she do if she loses her sedentary status? Could she be housed at my place without me risking the same punishment?

It's true that there's no law forbidding sedentary people to get together, or even to live side by side if they live in the same building, or to share accommodation; they just don't do it. All these emotions are so foreign to them that they decide, without consulting each other, not to mention them. How can you describe a feeling you can't even define?

Sunday for believers
A sunday show sponsored by léseN

*S*ince last night, disturbing documents have been circulating on the Internet, confirming the theory that Jesus did not die on the cross. The documents were allegedly stolen during a daring attack on the Vatican papal compound by the anti-globalization group Ubuntu a few months ago. The pontiff's inner circle is vigorously contesting their legitimacy, and the originals, sent by an anonymous courier to the relevant authorities, will shortly be analyzed to determine their age and relevance.

If they prove to be true, over 2,000 years of Judeo-Christian morality and doctrine will vanish, leaving billions of believers to fend for themselves.

" … The beauty of it, my dear, is that no one is forced to take the Jouvence capsules. And of those who do or will take them, none will ever be obliged to attend the parties organized by the sperm banks. And of those who do attend, none will be obliged to go every night."

Pierre, who now presents himself as the personal assistant to one of the most powerful figures in this progressive society, had understood all the subtleties of the Machiavellian mechanisms put in place by Nucleus, his mentor. He played with them with delight: that is the power of free will. The president of the investors' foundation is willing to set the scene, to suggest, to orchestrate even, if necessary, but never to impose.

"He who imposes puts himself in danger," he adds, paraphrasing Nucleus. He will be the one to point the finger to when things go wrong, the one who will be accountable. "With Jouvence, we offer health and youth to a sick humanity. We are, quite simply, its benefactors. What individuals do with this health and youth is their own business. We're even prepared to organize a major information campaign on the dangers of bus parties. Big deal! The dangers of busing?" he repeats, getting carried away by his own lyricism. "But who's going to be convinced? What's left to do, what's left for them?

Pierre circles around his interlocutor like a vulture circles its prey, waiting for her to perish. She belong to him, he knows it, but he prefers to delay the moment he already savors in advance. He wants to convince her first.

"To pray? God is dead. We have ended his long agony with the help of our precious "Ubuntu" enemies. Jesus died in his bed. He is not the son of God, just an enlightened carpenter who doubled as a great orator. It's proven. I'm sure they've started selling the furniture at the Vatican.

46

Pierre moves slowly toward her, piercing her with his eagle-like gaze, but she does not lower her eyes. He resumes his demonstration.

"Working? How many people in the history of work have been able to boast of combining a fascinating activity with a decent income? Just a handful! And most of them end up swelling the ranks of the big, beautiful Foundation chaired by my employer.

"By the way my dear, do you remember your elementary school lessons? Our predecessors, under the feudal system in Europe were proud to lead a "château life," working hard by the sweat of someone else's brow, in the name of aristocratic descent, of which they were the happy beneficiaries. Then, with the advent of the bourgeoisie, workers replaced serfs, but little really changed. When corporations held the reins of the economy, the vast majority of the working population swelled the profits of the few big investors, but now it's the banks that control society and major social advances.

"As soon as the global financial system allowed it, and money began to generate its own profits in sufficient proportions, the Investors' foundation found a way to do away with the *duty to* work to avoid competition and the economic need to produce and, therefore, consume. We've known all this for a long time, it comes at the detriment of our planet, whose limited resources could not indefinitely support these ferocious appetites. No more *duty* to work then, but a *right to* work. You won't argue with me that this work is as often useless and distressing as possible, but it is also essential, since it is a prerequisite for the *right to housing*.

Pierre no longer walks; he flies He spreads his arms like a theater actor at the end of a performance, when thunderous applause makes him lose all sense of proportion. Suddenly, he lowers his voice and almost whispers in the ear of his audience of one.

Love? There's no more family, no more landmarks, no more dating. Everything can be delivered to the house or obtained on the Internet. And the air is far too polluted and the sun is too dangerous for people to really want to go out more than once or twice in their lives. The air from the new air-conditioners is so good for those who can afford it! Without dating, without parents, there's no love. Two more generations and I'm telling you, it won't even be mentioned in the textbooks anymore.

Finally, it's the climax, the finishing blow. Pierre takes a few steps back. He holds off the rest of his demonstration just a bit longer than necessary, simply because he can. He takes another deep breath and concludes.

"All they've got left is sex, my dear, good old sex. The one that has always been at the center of everything: laws, morals, frustrations, transcendence, religions, art and Big Brother ads. Now that none of that remains, it's finally taking its rightful place, which it has always claimed with varying degrees of success since the dawn of time: it's the meaning of life.

"Unfortunately, to our great concern, humanity has lost its energy and with it the desire to frolic. That's why we've created Jouvence. Isn't the most beautiful death to die of pleasure?"

Pierre is at the height of ecstasy. He's smiling like an angel; his gaze is that of a man possessed, and his voice still echoes under the great archway of his employer's conservatory when he pauses to catch his breath and drink a glass of water. He stubbornly and deliberately refuses to utter the name of "the dear friend" in question, in order to make her feel even more insignificant.

Catherine stands speechless in front of the remarkable man; this is more than she's heard in her entire life. She should be worried and fearful for her future or even her life, but for the first time, someone who has no interest in lying and who has first-hand information confirms what she has always sensed; instead, she gloats! She's always known, she's always felt that the world doesn't run smoothly, and now she has the proof. Only yesterday, holed up in her little sedentary apartment, she was feeding her thoughts and doubts on the virtual pages collected by her Big Brother, which she hid away like a shameful treasure. She's not afraid anymore, she knows.

To Winston, she was crazy. An enjoyable fool, but a fool, nonetheless. "He'll see who's crazy!" she says to herself. She's proud, she's happy. She doesn't let herself be fooled like all the sedentary people. Even Winston fell for it, not her. NOT HER.

In the sidereal immensity of her uselessness, this dear friend was accumulating questions on all the subjects Pierre Banet had just raised. This remarkable orator and presumably extremely powerful man had done her the grace of inviting her to his home. How had he come to know of her existence? The emissary who had come to her and summoned her had made no secret of his superior's intentions.

"He wished to meet this sedentary woman who seemed to be asking such pertinent questions about the organization of society, the future of the planet and of mankind."

Instead, up until now, Catherine had listened more than anything else, without really realizing that access to her computer was supposed to be protected. She reveled in this hemorrhaging confession, which brought together the information and questions she'd been asking herself all her life. In the mouth of this important man, the destiny of mankind takes on the shape of a cathedral: in successive strata, each illustration, each sculpture, each stone tells a story. Together, they form an elegant, powerful, inescapable whole. As if standing before monuments that defied time.

Catherine is transfixed.

We're all going to die! She thinks, not allowing this fateful thought to ruin her joy of knowledge. She can't wait to share her new knowledge with Winston.

"Would you allow me to include this information in my next report? May I know your name…to cite my sources?" she advances.

Pierre simply answers "No" and shoots her in the head with his revolver, at point-blank range.

A sense of dread, or at least what he assumed was dread based on what he'd heard, when he arrived on his doorstep to find Catherine's door closed. It had become a kind of coded message between them that Winston had taken a long time to see, then to understand; an invitation in the form of a subliminal message: She leaves her door ajar as an invitation. On mornings when he's too exhausted, he gently closes it and goes home, but today he would have given anything for it to be open.

He tries in vain to reassure himself. *Maybe the door closed by itself* or *she fell asleep before opening the door.*

Nothing calms his nerves, but he can't bring himself to knock on the door and risk waking her, because she's probably asleep. In any case, he's too tired, his eyes urge him to let them close, which he finally concedes as he enters his office apartment.

A few hours later, an infernal racket in the corridor jolts him awake. He hadn't had time to take Jouvence this morning. Despite the overpowering fatigue that multiplies the force of gravity in his environment tenfold, he straightens up in one movement and finds himself on his feet. He is shaken by a terrible back pain as he moves toward his door.

Delivery persons are installing a complete refit of Catherine's apartment. A bed and night table, a dining room table and two chairs, a sofa and coffee table, a bookshelf and three paintings. Winston has never seen anything like it. Sometimes a sedentary person moves, but this is the first time, as far as he knows, that an apartment has been completely refurnished. It's government practice to let furniture gather dust before anyone decides to replace it. He also knows that Catherine doesn't have the financial means for such an investment.

Devoured by anxiety and curiosity, Winston opens his door wide, giving him a clearer view of what's going on: the apartment has been completely emptied and repainted. All in a night or two at the most. Granted, it's only been a few days since his last visit, but given the current bustle, there's no way the apartment could have been emptied without him noticing.

"Please return to your accommodation. I would like to remind you that it is strongly recommended by the Ministry of Welfare that you only go out on urgent errands and never for more than twenty-five minutes, twice a year, at most. Any offenders may have their social security cover withdrawn and be required to pay the full amount of any medical and hospital expenses that may arise." The delivery person's tone, filtered through his protective suit, is polite but unequivocal, and Winston complies without the slightest hesitation.

Catherine's gone; she's gone. It's not possible!

Instantly, his neighbor's paranoid theories comes to his mind. She has been removed by the authorities, who were able to get their hands on her texts or bypass her scrambler and access her web searches.

Catherine was right, the sedentary people are hamsters, spinning the invisible wheel installed in their prison cells to give them the illusion of escape. His heart was racing and his chest felt too tight for it. There was something happening to him, even his vision was altered by whatever this feeling was that was taking over his body. He is furious and would like to break it all up, but he can't risk being indicted thanks to the testimony of sworn delivery person.

So Winston remains prostrate, sitting on his bed and staring into space until silence returns behind his closed door.

He did nothing, he said nothing; he clung to his sedentary status, like vermin to the hair and pubic hair of the homeless.

Winston spends the months following that sinister day searching for Catherine on the Net during working hours. On the buses, every night, he watches helplessly as the actors mingle, turning over inert bodies in the early hours of the morning, terrified that he might recognize her. But she's nowhere to be seen, she's disappeared.

In the apartment, a new tenant moved in before the paint was completely dry, and the hunted-beast looks and eyes of his new neighbor immediately reminded Winston that solitude was his only companion.

Press release from the Ministry of Welfare

Some of our Freedom Army soldiers have agreed to take part in a scientific experiment that could well revolutionize medicine as we know it. They have agreed to allow the introduction of a neural electronic element, which could enable the establishment of an absolutely infallible health system. The intention is, in a second phase, to extend this protocol to the entire sedentary population. This would provide them with unprecedented medical coverage that could considerably reduce the Ministry of Welfare's budget and allow it to be used to support the war effort in the privatized territories of Africa.

These nanotechnological chips, known as "vital chips[i]," are likely to replace PEAR and ANDROGENE watches. They have the special feature of being able to communicate directly with the medical computers we use every day online, without any connection being necessary. They are likely to inform mutual health insurance companies, in real time, about the evolution of their policyholders' illnesses, and diagnose—and then treat and cure, of course—any abnormality before it becomes fatal. Great hopes are being pinned on curing people of diseases that were previously incurable.

Let's pay tribute to our glorious freedom fighters for their courage and sense of duty.

The lives of Nucleus and his kind are very different from those of sedentary people:

They live in couples, have social relationships with their peers, professional motivations and children who remind them of what it means to love one's neighbor, if that neighbor is of the same social condition, of course.

They live in seclusion, sheltered from the sedentary population, in little paradises called "Eden," which have developed identically in financially strategic parts of the globe. They live on the edge of a society they have created, just as others created counterfeit money in their day, stamped with the effigy of their sick thirst for power. The strongest, the fittest and most powerful have survived since the dawn of time.

The Edenians could have taken advantage of scientific advances in reproduction to improve their offspring by selecting their best genes, but why go against nature when nature has already been so generous? Of course, children are not born by Edenians, but by sedentary females, whom they choose from a catalog. As for the rest, nature does things well.

These winners live surrounded by gigantic, impenetrable polymethyl methacrylate bubbles that protect them from the climatic hazards of global warming, the sun's deadly rays and the air pollution for which they and their descendants are responsible. And yet, they are the only ones still able to enjoy outdoor activities.

"Daddy, look, I've drawn you a picture." Christ, the son of Nucleus, has a real gift, and everything he reproduces literally seems to come to life on paper.

"That's good, darling," replies his father, stroking his hair mechanically. "Go and show it to your mother, I'm rereading what your sister has just written for her tutor."

Nucleus has very little time for his family, but he devotes almost all of it to Electra J., his beloved daughter.

"She's really full of ideas, that little girl," he thinks aloud, not paying attention to his little boy as he goes back to his room with his head bent.

Once the door has closed on his kingdom, Christ carefully picks up the metal box that he's hidden under his bed.

It's poorly hidden, in case his father decides to take interest in him enough to find it. It's filled with the items he's most proud of, the ones he wants his father to find.

He opens the lid with some form of ceremony and places inside it the extraordinary portrait of Nucleus that he has just made.

For an eight-year-old, this is absolutely remarkable.

In this miniature vault lies the many tokens of a child's affection for his father, buried by him like so many orphaned, stillborn bastards.

He closes and replaces his treasure in its hiding place, grabs one of his countless balls and storms out of his room.

"What are you doing, Christ?" asks Aurore, his mother, as she sees him stroll into one of the living rooms. "How many times have I asked you not to play ball in the house? You could damage one of your father's icons, and you know he'd never forgive you."

"I'm not playing, Mum, I'm going outside."

"In that case, go slower, sweetie… I'll tell your sister to join you as soon as she's finished with your father."

Christ waits for what seems like an eternity before the carefree Electra J. deigns to appear in the garden.

"Will you play with me?" he asks her so softly. Without waiting for an answer to a question his sister can't have heard, the little boy throws the ball in her face, almost at point-blank range, with strength increased tenfold by the wait.

"Mommy, Mommy, Electra J. hurt herself with the ball, Mommy!"

Week after week, month after month, year after year, busers fill the ever-increasing number of mobile brothels with their coital moans. Whether in Europe, the Grand Orient, or the United Amercas, every night these infernal rounds take place. In the cities, only the "seniors" seventy and over, confined to their medicalized residences, and persons under age don't take part. Many of them bitterly regret this and have to make do with the documentaries on the subject offered to them by their Big Brother. Children and especially teenagers, stuck in their individual school cells between a virtual classroom, a video game or a visit to SUB, hear about it on their screens. They are already dreaming of the day when they too can go. Despite the fears that each inspires in others, boredom and hormones bring the beast out of its lair when desire is stronger than reason.

In the case of consenting adults and the strict necessity of harvesting gametes, the respective governments laxly regulate an activity that stems directly from the concessions and indulgences made to Orson and Orson. It also allows them to channel the crowds.

Isn't the old saying that sex is the cure for all diseases? Or maybe it's love…

The law prohibits more than two visits per week, but there are far too many buses to enforce this regulation properly. Gradually, and in view of the many deaths that have occurred on sperm bank transports, Jouvence capsules have been declared a "controlled medication," but anyone can obtain them cheaply on the Internet. Incessant campaigns are organized to make sedentary people aware of the serious risks of exhaustion, up to and including death, that offenders can suffer, but who cares?

Despite all this, for many sedentary people, after days employed in useless and debilitating work, every evening is an incredible adventure, never the same people on the same buses, never the same themes. At first, Winston was content to be a spectator when a theme seemed more deviant than he liked, but it was impossible for him to resist for long before such debauches of lust, scent and offered flesh. Like everyone else, he ended up tasting everything.

Little by little, the buses have become more sophisticated. More spacious and more comfortable, they offered everyone everything they needed to facilitate ejaculation and harvest oocytes under analgesia. If a machine was more effective than traditional bodily stimuli, we had the choice of using the machine. Just as cows used to be milked, males suffering from erectile dysfunction can now connect their penis to a vibrating latex sucker that makes even the most recalcitrant howl with pleasure.

As for women, they've not been forgotten. After harvesting their oocytes, they're all shot up with Jouvence, chaining orgasms together in the same way that athletes, in the days when the air was breathable, chained hurdles together over one hundred and ten meters. Always under tension, always on the verge of succumbing, they're perpetually on the verge of orgasm, and when, exhausted, they have to pause, it's with trembling bodies, victims of the attacks of a clitoris never satiated. Their whole bodies are subjugated to pleasure: their hands enjoy the penises they grasp, which harden under their protrusions, their mouths swell with the joy of tasting penises or expanding vulvas, their breasts rise under repeated and pressing assaults, their assholes hammered and offered to all and sundry overflow with precious seeds escaped from the condoms that serve as makeshift vials. And when their cunts are in agony, it's their asses that make them articulate the most beautiful moans. The sedentary ones give themselves, lose themselves, and it's only then that they finally discover themselves. Once you've tasted such ecstasy, it's impossible to escape. Who could want to? Men or women, when the jailer's caresses are infinitely sweeter than those of freedom, who will choose freedom?

56

Electra J.'s mother is a gentle, discreet and self-effacing woman, but she is powerfully intuitive and endowed with intellectual resources of which she is completely unaware. She has devoted her entire life to supporting her husband when he calls on her, but all too often, too, to making excuses for him when his attitude or actions become inexcusable.

Nucleus does not spare her. She is to him like the priest or therapist of centuries past. He tells her everything, hiding nothing from her for as long as they've known each other.

Nucleus and Aurore met very young. As children, born in the same Eden residence, they grew up together, and later frequented the same circles.

Aurore's elegant, vapid bearing combined with the depth of her family's bank account had turned the heads of many a suitor, even the wealthiest, but no one could move her like Nucleus.

He was at once respectful of propriety and continually thought outside the box; deeply romantic, he could sometimes show complete indifference toward others; charming and implacable; artistic and fragile as a child, powerful as a wildcat, the teenager had grown up to become a formidable businessman.

She'd fallen in love with him long before she knew it, and he was far too busy rethinking the world to pay her the attention she needed. To him, she was simply his confidant, his advisor and his stooge too, for he loved more than anything the envious looks of others when she was on his arm.

When they finally became lovers, the only thing that changed radically was the physical happiness one gave to the other. In these intimate moments, Nucleus once again became the infinitely gifted artist his childhood had given him a glimpse of. Aurora was the ever-surprising canvas on which he painted tirelessly, and which inspired him a little more every day.

She was an astute witness to all the major social changes inspired by the man who became her husband: the lifetime wage, online medicine and justice, education and government-sponsored retirement. She saw the most prestigious heads of state parade through the antechamber of their home to take advice, ask for support or bow to the decisions of the foundation of which Nucleus gradually became president. His actions commanded respect and admiration. Aurore's love knew no bounds.

After the birth of their two children, their eldest daughter, Electra J., soon showed talents inherited from the best of both parents. Adorable, discerning, meticulous and persevering. A free spirit, admired above all by both her mother and father. Curious about everything, she had a thirst for discovery, and this urgency was matched only by her admiration for her father. Her dream was that he could be her tutor, rather than the people her parents imposed on her, always different, but so much alike and for whom she had so little esteem. There are some things that children can only learn or even understand later on, and Nucleus didn't want to bother with this preliminary step, so he had chosen teaching accordingly: SUBs could only share with their pupils what had been implanted in their clone brains and which was only a watered down, purified and reworked version of art, literature, history and the workings of society.

The finest minds can only really question what they know, and Electra J. was not yet old enough to grasp the economic and political mechanisms her father had made his daily life.

"Mom, why can't we leave the bubble?" asks Electra J. to Aurore as they were silently gazing the sunbeams playing with the texture of the dome.

"My dear, the air outside is unhealthy and prolonged contact with the earth can cause illness. We don't want you or your brother to risk your health for something that isn't worth it. I've shown you photos of what the earth was like before the great upheavals, and your father is doing everything he can to make up for the mistakes of the past, but for the moment it's not possible."

"Did people do bad things? Is that what daddy has to fix?"

"Yes, darling, people have made mistakes and there are too many of them for things to get better any time soon. Outside the walls of our residence, there are far too many dangers."

2069:
Winston

For ten years I've been taking Jouvence. Why did I start? I can hardly remember. I was satisfied, it seems and lacked nothing. I seem to remember that I was exhausted and terrorized by others before I met Catherine. She has almost become my soulmate. It sounds ridiculous as I write it, but I almost fell for it back then and now I can barely remember what was so important to me. All I remember are empty and useless words, empty feelings that pollute the mind and prevent me from concentrating on my work and pleasure. The morning she was gone, I almost fell for the plot. I looked for her on all the buses at night and all over the Net during the day. When I learned that she'd accepted the job at the Ministry of Work Distribution that had been offered to me, I realized just how much I'd been fooled. From then on, only desire, the desire to come and the need to come kept my rage at bay. When all that surrounds such intense sexual pleasure is gray, pale, tasteless routine, I've discovered on the buses that powerful smells aren't necessarily repulsive, nor the potential danger posed by insurmountable sedentary others. So what there's more to discover? A stunning "elsewhere"? Do all the sedentary people I pass in the evenings, with whom I've exchanged nothing but cries and grumbles, also feel this pain that's so hard to define?

How can we know when we don't speak? How can we speak if words have no meaning? Now I think I've been profoundly unhappy. How can we conceptualize this idea with words that are no longer defined by the meaning they were originally given? Sometimes they even mean the opposite: happiness, plenitude, risk, taste, well-being, even democracy, security, freedom, great social advances and celebration. I'm not sure what they mean or what they imply.

The party… But that's exactly why I decided to take part in the bus parties. To forget my interminable days, to live intensely and to get a little extra money.

I'm beginning to doubt that too. Of course, I don't talk about it with anyone. I won't be asked again, and no one will dare to come and talk to me about it because of all the fuss and lawsuits in the media. However, I'm certain that none of the busers who joined the parties had any other idea than to have a good time. And it's happiness that drives people to party, and it's despair that drives the weakest to suicide, isn't it? If that's the case, I can't explain what happened last night when I caught my bus much later than usual.

As I entered, I quickly realized that the party was already well underway. People were everywhere, and as usual, no one was talking to anyone. But what the hell, they were fucking, smelling of sperm and sweat despite the synthetic perfumes and incense. I hadn't been there for at least three days. It must be said that the time before, I'd almost died there and there were nearly twenty deaths on my bus alone. It was really disgusting; I'm very close to the terminus and every time it's me who takes the morbid walk. Most of the time, the corpses are blue, their eyes and mouths wide open. In my opinion, these idiots suffocate to death. That or a heart attack because I've nearly had one on several occasions. And all those chicks who have orgasms lasting several hours, that's got to wear them out too. Anyway, I decided to take it easy. I spot a fit young woman in one of the showers, not very tall, but super toned and, in my opinion, very attractive. I'm glad, because most of the time, they're rather stunted and flabby. After putting my clothes away in the locker, I approach her. I have to admit that I quickly forgot my tiredness and my good resolutions in the face of so many arguments.

Even in isolated corners, it's not easy to get along with all those guys and gals shouting and the music blasting. But I could see she was breathing hard from the speed at which her tits and belly were moving. All dripping with the water that had just gone off, her skin was taking on the changing colors of the psychedelic lights, and I was already hard as a bull. I'd never done a girl on my own before, and I must admit I was tempted. This time, there was no doubt who was going to make her come. I run my hand gently over her belly and immediately feel her react. Her skin is soft and burning. Without looking at me—but that's normal, no one looks at anyone on the bus—she arches her back and gives me a glimpse of the promise of a beardless, supple, toned pussy. I take her two gorgeous pale-pink nipples by storm, one in my mouth and the other in my hand, and feel them harden in my embrace. I lick her belly and drink everything in it, right up to the entrance to her sex. For once, I'm not going to throw myself in headfirst. So I admire them and tease it with my tongue. That's nature's well done; it opens up immediately, revealing the slight reverberation so characteristic of a well-lubricated vagina. I borrow one of my hands from one of her breasts to spread her already docile labia and gain easier access to her clitoris. It's electric and her belly moves in unison with my licks. I finally hear her moan above the general hubbub. I don't change position or technique until her cry of deliverance has sounded, and I must say it doesn't take long.

This time, even more than the others, it was impossible to distinguish the expression on her face at the moment of orgasm from the one she might have had if I'd beaten her to death. These are the mysteries of pleasure.

I then slide my saliva-moistened finger into her vagina and rotate her around this axis so that, on her stomach, she can offer me her ass to devour. All clean, wet and second handedly lubricated, I dilate it with my tongue without ceasing to masturbate her. She takes the initiative and pulls herself up onto my lap. Thus offered, I have to accept and humbly present my penis at the gates of her pleasures. She chooses to engulf me in her cunt, and I'm delighted, taking the opportunity to massage her dilated anus with my thumb. After a few more thrusts, she cries out again. A woman for yourself is really very pleasant. I turn her over again with the firm intention of finally freeing myself in the reservoir of my condom. I push her legs up to her chest and multiply my options, I decide to surprise her with a different kind of penetration. Her supple, firm ass welcomes me in triumph and hugs the shape of my exploring penis. I think it was at this precise moment that I lost my sense of time and measure. A metronome without time or measure that beat to the rhythm of my pleasure the surroundings of her femininity. I could hear nothing but my own breathing and the orders of pleasure that were slow in coming. She was sweating profusely, I think, and her clenched hands on either side of her thighs were inviting me on a journey, leading the way. As the semen drained from my sex, I was able to follow its entire journey from my balls to the reservoir in my mind. I screamed like I rarely do. Short of breath, with a slight indisposition in my chest, I stayed like that until my deflated sex left its sheath, and then our eyes met: she was dead. I stand still for a moment, torn between the bliss characteristic of full and consummate enjoyment and the unpleasant surprise of my involuntary necrophilia. I decide to put some distance between myself and the inert body, staggering backward. Leaving the shower room, I stumble over another body, then a third. I lose my balance and land limply on the still-warm corpses of the night's pleasure seekers. No, this one's not dead. He looks at me haggardly, desperate to catch his breath, his chest shaking with macabre hiccups. I sit up straight, dreading this tide of dying and dead bodies as much as I can.

In the end, I'll be the only one to leave the bus tonight.

"Mr. President, I thank you for the honor of coming to visit me in person today," declares Nucleus as he storms into the small salon of his sumptuous home. There, the president of the European Cartel, Salvadore Empuña, awaits him. "To what do I owe the pleasure of seeing you, and what can I do to please you?"

Finishing his sentence as if he'd begun it before even opening the door, Nucleus takes possession of his host's hand with the attitude of one who wishes to keep it as a trophy.

"I have far too little time for your mundanities, Orson," continues the politician, rising to his feet and in a tone that stands in definite contrast to the lightness of tone suggested by Nucleus.

"If I'm compelled to come here, it's because you refused to meet the spokesman I'd delegated to conclude the matter at hand," escalates Empuña, betrayed by his Spanish accent, which takes some of the coldness out of his tone.

"Speaking of spokesmen, allow me to introduce my assistant, Pierre, whom I don't think you've met yet."

Pierre had remained cautiously on the doorstep, waiting to be invited to come or go.

"I've already heard of him. It's quite surprising to learn that you're recruiting from the sedentary population now," replies the president without a glance toward the interested party.

Pierre stands his ground.

Nucleus did not doubt for a moment that the President had made his inquiries before moving and sat down on one of the sumptuous sofas in the small lounge without inviting the President to do the same.

"I have the weakness of thinking that we share the same points of view and that you believe, as I do, that talent is not reserved for the highest classes of our society."

"I think so, but I'm surprised to hear that's your opinion too," replies the diplomat, continuing without a moment's pause. "I have some documents I'd like you to sign."

Empuña places a clipboard on the table between himself and the Nucleus chair.

"It's about Jouvence, of course, and how the product was introduced to the market," replies Nucleus. "On this matter, I have with me another document that I would like to submit to your kind attention."

Nucleus gives Pierre a very slight wave of the hand, and he enters the diplomatic battlefield without hesitation, handing the President what he had kept preciously in his hands.

"This is an acknowledgement of assets that I have diligently transferred to an offshore account opened in your name at one of my partners' banks."

"Ten million WVU? But I've never asked you for anything," snaps the first man in European's Cartel.

"But every effort deserves its reward, Mr. President, and I'd like to thank you very much for the facilities you've kindly granted our new product."

"I won't sign any IOUs—the money is too much like a bribe for me to accept. Besides, your product is starting to wreak havoc with the sedentary population, and I can't tolerate it, let alone stand by and do nothing."

"Unfortunately, Mr. Chairman, whether you sign the acknowledgement or not, this money is and will remain in an account that belongs to you. What you do with it is none of my business. I would, however, like to reiterate my unconditional support for your policy, and you can now take for granted the full financial strength of my group when the difficult period of election campaigns comes around," he concludes by way of a final blow.

Empuña looks at Nucleus with eyes full of the surprise like someone who had just been stabbed, and prepares to leave the room, neglecting the document Pierre hands him.

"By the way, Mr. President, from now on, I'll be grateful if you got in touch with my assistant for all the things we'll be doing together in the very near future. I wish to withdraw from day-to-day business and entrust him with the management of minor affairs."

When Empuña leaves the scene furious and defeated, Nucleus turns to Pierre.

"You see, it's not rocket science; we have them by the balls anyway. You're going to indulge me doing the same with the other puppets from the Orient and the Americas."

"Are you bored? Want to watch a show on Big Brother?" Electra J. speaks to her doll in the same way her mother speaks to her, with a voice full of love and attention. She knows she's not allowed to turn on the Multimedia Complex, but she's not doing it for herself, she's doing it for her bored doll. So they both head for the device, which has been switched off for years and is tucked away in a corner of one of the rooms in the house where no one ever goes.

"I'll put you down on the sofa, don't move, I'll be right back. See, I'm right in front of you."

Electra J. has grabbed the remote control she found in one of the drawers of the multimedia cabinet, and is frantically pressing all the buttons, with nothing happening.

I promised my doll I'd do it, she thinks.

Looking down at the Big Brother from her nine-year-old perspective, Electra J. notices that the device isn't connected. She's not sure what that means, but she knows from watching others do it that when you connect a device, it starts working. She looks for and finds the pad on which to move the device to make contact, and a small red light appears below the screen. Electra J. tries again to press the remote control buttons, but nothing happens.

This time, it's personal. Electra J. is methodical, diligent and a little stubborn. These are, of course, qualities that her parents recognize in her and that make Nucleus so proud of his daughter. Suddenly, the remote control seems very light, and she wonders if it needs a battery to work, like her doll. She looks at her doll and her doll looks at her. She's well aware that she's no longer doing all this just for herself, but the desire to overcome difficulties is stronger than anything. She approaches her toy gently, turns it over slowly so that it doesn't notice, and with a quick movement opens the case. She extracts the battery that powers it. She knows that all she can do now is sleep and certainly not watch what's going on with Big Brother, but she also knows that this battery may be the solution to all her problems. She reaches for the remote control again, opens it and inserts what she has just removed from her doll. A little red light immediately appears on the remote control when she presses the button, sitting on the sofa next to her inert doll, and Big Brother's black screen lights up almost instantly. She's very proud of herself, and she knows her daddy would be very proud of her too. On media channels, competition is fierce. Every programmer has long since done away with any self-censorship when it comes to violence or sex. The important thing is to excite and shock the audience rather than inform or entertain them. The first images Electra J. sees on the big screen are those of an exhaustive report on bus activities. Although she doesn't quite understand the presenter's comments, what she sees is definitely not appropriate for her age, and she quickly realizes this. However, just as an electrocuted person cannot detach himself from the cable that is inescapably bringing him down, Electra J. cannot look away from what is before her eyes. The report goes on and on, describing the orgies, but also the corpses piling up on the buses and in the streets when the maintenance staff can't cope with the task. But it's the next story that no child her age could have borne. It describes in detail what is happening in the privatized territories of Africa, where the Grand Orient, Europe and the United States share the continent's wealth and fuel internal wars, under the guise of fighting the terrorist group Ubuntu. She sees children torn apart by machine-gun fire at point-blank range, parents crushed under ruined walls weakened by bombardments, mothers raped, fathers tortured and thrown into mass graves. The images follow one another like horror in overdrive, but her mind no longer receives them, her gaze is fixed, she is no longer there, she hides deep in her brain so as not to see anymore.

Today, Nucleus discovered his daughter watching the news on a forgotten Big Brother in a lost corner of the house. She was forbidden to use it, and it was supposed to be out of order anyway.

Why this ban? To protect her from the horrors of the world, and to shield her from the damaging effects of information dedicated entirely to brainwashing those who submit to it. Who else, but the one who possesses the tools of this information, controls it and shapes it, to judge it at its true value?

"How could I have imagined that in such a privileged setting, sedentary people would indulge in such depraved, sordid and suicidal games that endanger their lives and the very equilibrium of our society?" murmurs Nucleus in the ear of his motionless daughter completely unable to hear or even understand these adult words. "My darling, I could never have imagined it, don't blame me, I had nothing to do with it, my darling, I had nothing to do with it…". In the living room, the holographic screen reproduces in three dimensions the unprecedented slaughter taking place in every Cartel City and in the privatized territories in Africa. The eight wall-mounted speakers relay and amplify the terrifying cacophony, completing the picture in 3D. Humans are dying by the millions around her, on buses, in the streets and in Africa. Their corpses pile up in huge infernos that obscure the horizon with thick black smoke.

Electra J. is nine years old, has never been outside Eden and has never been in contact with anyone other than the very privileged members of her community. Until now, she hadn't watched any of the programs offered on Big Brother. She knew nothing about megacities, sedentary people, Jouvence and busers, or what goes on in the privatized territories of Africa. Her parents, like the parents of the entire community, were utterly uncompromising on this point. So she spent most of her time in the company of the SUB, her friends and neighbors.

"I should never have left a Multimedia Complex in this house," moans Nucleus. "It's ridiculous, it's been so long since that device had been used, I'd completely forgotten about it."

Her father carries her to her room. Her eyes are fixed on the void, her body heavy. What she has seen is beyond what she could ever have imagined. For her, the little protege of all proteges, the shock has been very severe, she shows no sign of consciousness, and her eyes reflect the staggering depth of her incomprehension. She now lies on her bed, her mother at her bedside, in tears, and her father stammers out whatever comes to mind. He tries to retrace, for his petrified, little daughter, the history of the company he has repeatedly boasted to her of being the decisive architect.

In the space of just a few months, there's been a massacre on the buses. Every evening, thousands of busers' bodies pile up.

After six months, with more than four thousand deaths per city per day, the central governments of the Far East, Europe and the United Americas were caught unawares. They declared a general curfew, banned bus traffic and withdrew Jouvence's operating visa, which had initially been granted under pressure from the investors' foundation.

This in no way slows down the process.

The need to live, to enjoy, is stronger than all the prohibitions, all the repression and all the laws: the lack that motivates it is stronger than anything. Sex to the point of exhaustion. Sex as a last resort against boredom, despair, isolation and a meaningless future. Nobody talks about suicide. There's talk of victims, of a plot hatched by "Ubuntu."

The "Jouvencers" now know each other better, and although there will never be any question of trust between them, when they communicate to decide on the next meeting place, they do so without going through their Big Brother. They circumvent Jouvence's ban by using the parallel counterfeit networks that are springing up in every city and think of themselves as outlaws. They are called revolutionaries on political broadcasts. No longer sedentary or Jouvencers, the media call them "Busers," and naively, they take a certain pride in this. They have the confused feeling that they have made their destiny their own, that they can finally choose their life, even if it means dying for it.

Governments could never have imagined the power of such a resolution.

On Big Brothers, they are described as real terrorists who jeopardize the order and safety of the other members of the community. They are effectively disenfranchised when the delivery drivers manage to discover their meeting places in time. Dead busers become the victims of attacks, and busers who are still active become traitors to be denounced and fought.

However, the Jouvencers never had any intention of fighting against a power that, they always think, protects them. Instead, they fight against the boredom and isolation of a too-protected, too-dull life. As they turn on their Big Brother on sober evenings, they fail to understand the reasons why the media spreads such lies about them. They stubbornly refuse to acknowledge the limitations of their confined existence, failing to consider that the very institutions they still hold dear could be the cause of their discontent. How could they, they have no point of comparison?

And every night the mass graves reappear.

The sperm bank buses are requisitioned to collect the corpses. The delivery workers, the only ones authorized to circulate in the streets, are transformed into both forces of law and order, which until now had become useles, and a morticians. Every day, they come and go under the Jouvencers 'windows, who will do their utmost to be part of the next batch when the night comes.

Continuously, the automatic cranes of the "Ministry of Solidarity" fill the buses, whose roofs have been removed to facilitate loading and avoid the risk of infection.

Automatic crematoria carbonize the busers' bodies at infernal rates, but the task is far too monumental to be accomplished properly, and all over the city, bodies are rotting in the open air.

It's in this infectious breeding ground that, every night, more Jouvencers come to die of pleasure. Those who survive their sexual exploits end up dying of diseases contracted in mass graves, which they cannot report online for fear of being denounced.

For many decades now, governments, covered by debts contracted by private banking institutions to repay the colossal interest on loans contracted by themselves in previous years, have abandoned the budgets inherent in the army and, more generally, in defense.

These decisions were presented as magnificent advances for humanity and the planet. This is undoubtedly true, but the motivations are quite different.

In the first place, all countries are now so politically and economically linked that contemplating war was as absurd as taking a hammer to break a limb.

Of course, the global economy is not deprived of the benefits of conflict; it's just that it's all taking place in Africa. Terrible, murderous fratricidal wars are bleeding the continent and have continued and even intensified since privatization. In order to finance their armies, African countries took out disproportionate and impossible-to-repay loans. The global military industry, backed by the banks, eventually agreed to write off previous debts in return for ceding territory. In this way, Cameroon, Congo, Nigeria and many others have become private territories on which the industries of the coalition countries are developing, in order to relocate polluting industries to Africa.

African countries, at war all the time, are far too weakened economically, demographically and politically to ever imagine being a threat to major economic entities.

Funding for regular armies has thus disappeared from the budgets of the three superpowers.

Of course, all private armies now depend in one way or another on funding from members of the Investor Foundation.

In a way, the Foundation is the only military power on the planet.

By the time governments decide to ask for help from the private armies of freedom, which until then had been deployed entirely in Africa, nearly four billion sedentary people from the three Cartels have already died.

Nucleus is more determined than ever to see his project through. What happened to his daughter must never happen again, to any of his family. She will be forever scarred by the memory of that experience, and he will never forgive himself. He invested an infinite amount of time over several years, using all his connections and all his financial influence to ensure that this new version of the "Patriot Act" would see the light of day. Above all, he wanted it to be passed by all the countries that make up the three economic powers. He used all his energy and determination, even at the risk of seeing his role revealed. After all, how can we explain the fact that, for the first time in modern human history, all parties of all ideological persuasions are in agreement?

The support of the members of the Investor Foundation who own and run the media was decisive.

And then, in the end, it doesn't matter to him. After decades of compromises that have enabled the Foundation to control all the political, economic, financial and religious stakes, he could almost come out into the open. Almost... The planet is still too densely populated to risk an uprising so close to the goal.

Even though power and might are the inextricable links that bind the members of the Foundation together, a few of them could disassociate themselves if they knew too many details. To really bring about such a change in society, it's essential that everyone involved knows as little as possible. As in the assembly line developed by Ford in his day, each person's skills must be used to the maximum and their intellectual skills to the minimum. This means that they do not know exactly what they are working on. This is the price we have to pay to avoid any existential crisis, political opposition or questioning of the partnerships without which nothing can really succeed. In a way, acting for the good of all without their knowledge. Unfortunately, this is what Nucleus has done all his life. And then, when the end is nigh, there will still be a few million sedentary people who will need to be kept around for a while to finally achieve the new world order he dreams of. These people will still be lucky enough to be able to settle on the bangs of the new system and live a little longer without fearing that their vital needs will run out. At least, they will be useful to the Nucleus project. It will be a handful, of course, on a planetary scale: many military personnel, a few hand-picked doctors and magistrates and show-business artists whose aura or expertise will always be indispensable to those who control them. Already, the medicine and law for the sedentary are being dispensed online by computers programmed with the help of the few doctors and lawyers, in the name of fair and homogeneous medicine and justice for all. To enjoy their loyalty in complete safety and avoid any hint of awareness or revolt, no one must ever know of Nucleus's decisive role in shaping the new world order. It must continue to provide them with the money and material goods that symbolize their ephemeral masquerade's success and prestige. These associates, who will still be lucky enough to enjoy these meager privileges, will see their ranks thinning soon enough, and eventually be too afraid of being part of the next "reshuffle" to stop collaborating.

What a wonderful system, he thinks.

As Nucleus knows only too well, the combination of the vital needs of food, shelter, clothing and social validation has always been a powerful force to drive people toward any kind of activity that might cause them, or their fellow human beings, to suffer.

In the 20th century, the specter of unemployment was even more terrifying for the masses than spending fifty years of their lives doing tasteless, underpaid work.

Until now, the sedentary population of the cartels has been regulated to the extent necessary for the production economy to sell its products. It is impossible to drastically reduce the population without risking a recession, at least as long as it is a production economy. Nucleus's plan is to replace the production economy with a financial economy, where money begets money without the inconvenience of consumption.

In any case, the new order will enable Nucleus to gradually get rid of all the surplus of "futureless" people around the world, who no longer serve any purpose and are polluting the planet with their vital demands.

The final stage of his scenario will take place in Africa. That's where he'll find everything he doesn't yet control: the big corporations that aren't members of the Foundation, and the OPEP production companies that produce everything consumer society, the weapon industry and the aeronautics industry could want. When all is said and done, these useless industries will cease to feed the market. However, Nucleus knows perfectly well that the surplus produced for the 12 billion humans will be more than enough for the one hundred and twenty million privileged people who will remain. No production, no pollution.

It's also in Africa that Nucleus and his ilk have isolated perpetual war, transforming every head office into a veritable fortress. This necessity, too, will become useless, and it will be from the ashes of this sacrificed continent that the utopia that Nucleus already calls, in the secret of his dearest hopes, Eden, will be born.

2074

Ten years have passed since Electra J.'s accident. She gradually regained her health and a normal life, but a part of her died that day, and her relationship with her father became infinitely more complicated. As a teenager, she realized that she could find no doctor, no psychiatrist, no friend who was anything other than a mouthpiece for her sire. Her brother has become cold and distant toward her since returning to the family home at the end of his long stay in a psychiatric clinic. They no longer speak to each other.

She ends up despising them all, looking elsewhere for support and understanding.

Only her mother still enjoys her love and admiration, but Electra J. suffers infinitely to see her so gloomy now and obviously unhappy and worried. Of course, she never mentions it and refuses to discuss it when Electra J. tries to broach the subject.

"Mom, tonight I've organized a videoconference where all the young Edenians from the various Cartel residences are invited. Well, you're not young enough to take part, but you can come and listen if you like?" she asks a little mischievously.

Aurore evades the question.

"You're really amazing, how you manage to do things like that. I wouldn't be able to get this many people together for any reason."

"You know, I'm not sure I'm going to unleash any passions today; they're all so jaded already and they're barely twenty."

"And what's the subject of this boring lecture? Jouvence, I presume?" she replies, changing her tone imperceptibly. "I wish you'd leave your father alone."

Electra J. darkens immediately.

"It's not about Nucleus this time or his miracle drug, I'd like to discuss with the other residents, the military government, martial law and the three-year state

75

of emergency. It was supposed to protect the sedentary, I think, and I don't get the impression that much has changed on that front…"

Aurore can feel it; Electra J. is about to broach the subject of Jouvence, and every time she does, the tone escalates, causing them both pain. This time, however, she can't see how to change the conversation.

Electra J. adds, "The Molecule of Jouvence is still being smuggled and is still wreaking havoc. We're told it's the busers, that the busers are dreadful terrorists who must be persecuted, but then, as far as I know, the buser's activity was organized by pharmaceutical companies and approved by governments, wasn't it? And the drug that caused the outbursts was Jouvence by Orson and Orson. Without your husband, busers would probably never have existed."

"Electra J, please stop calling your father *my husband*. Jouvence was originally a miracle drug that immediately transformed the lives of millions of sedentary people, but its use has been hijacked by perverts."

Electra J. picks up the pace.

"Did they? And why did these sedentary people need them so badly? And why did so few Edenians take them?"

"We're eating better and healthier, that's all. If some people prefer to spend their money against common sense rather than buy quality food, that's their problem. You can't blame your father for all the evils of the world," Aurore tries to conclude.

"Mom, don't you see that everything is linked? The living wage has enabled our banks to buy the lives of billions of people for the price of a few worthless figures cleverly placed in the accounts of those they needed to control.

"Mortified by the boredom of their solitary, pollution-cloistered existence in a hermetically sealed environment, graciously fed a substance that Father always refused to let us taste, what choices did these sedentary people have? What were their prospects? Their free education is nothing less than the first step in a large-scale formatting process that continues into adulthood, when society offers them housing and an insane, mind-numbing job. This housing is nothing less than the antechamber to the retirement home that awaits them. To speed up the passage of time, they have their own Multimedia Complex, which Nucleus has always forbidden us to watch, and for good reason, may I add, per my experience, and Jouvence to make the body exult."

"I can't let you say that," replies Aurore, desperate, tears rimming her grey eyes. "I was there for every decision your father made, he consulted me, I was enthusiastic about all the projects he initiated. It's true that your father has a lot of influence, but he's always made sure to use that influence for good. I can't let you attribute all these horrible schemes to him."

"I'm sorry, Mom, I'm not blaming you for anything. I just need to know, need to understand, need to talk and I can only do that with you. Christ never leaves his father and everyone else around us is a friend, acquaintance or employee of Nucleus."

Electra J. kisses her mother who continues to cry and holds her in her arms. It is so hard to see one's mother cry and even harder for Electra who caused it. She would like to erase their last conversation, but deep down, she knows it is Nucleus she is angry with. He is the one who makes her mother cry, not her.

"I have to go, Mom, I can't miss a meeting I've organized."

Sperm bank laboratory headquarters
– Privatized Liberia, Africa[iii]

The heavy weapons mounted atop the watchtowers surrounding the sperm bank's headquarters have finally fallen silent.

Even though research and defense infrastructure operate with very few personnel, only a handful of them choose to take part in the battle between the Army of Freedom and the African Revolutionary Armed Forces "UBUNTU" for sport and to beat boredom. Nevertheless, it is impossible to continue work when the laboratory is under siege, as all energy sources are neutralized for security reasons, but also to avoid any risk of sabotage.

Since the resumption of fighting between separatists from the privatized territories and the armies of freedom, production levels have dropped alarmingly at all industrial sites in Africa. Employees are very apprehensive about the forthcoming annual appraisals and the restructuring that will inevitably follow. Many of them, and no one here wants that, could be sent back to their sedentary conditions in the Cartel of their birth.

At the sperm bank laboratory, it's not a question of production or even storage as such, but of research, and the fighting considerably delays the work.

Mallence was born in Europe. Graceful and slender, she could, under other skies, have become an actress or model. Friedrich, less slender and balder than his age would suggest, comes from the United States. They've been an exceptional team since the start of their careers because they are at once radically different, almost opposite, and perfectly complementary, like the two parts of a cup and ball game.

They met in Africa, just after finishing their studies, in the laboratories of the sperm bank. Both born to anonymous parents and educated in sedentary boarding schools in their native Cartel, they set about developing new prototypes of SUB, Homo convertibilis.

Africa's highly unstable political and economic context, in which the workers have to survive and produce, makes interaction inevitable, and trust has gradually built up between them, despite their sedentary upbringing.

During these long periods of inaction, caused by the proximity of confrontations, Internet connections, like energy sources, are cut off most of the time, and conversation is the only alternative to combat and the only real remedy for fear.

Mallence is convinced that something radical is going on in the Cartels and that essential information about Big Brothers is not being revealed. Generally speaking, Mallence finds it hard to trust people, which is one of the reasons why she decided to join the Worker sector rather than the Sedentary one. On the other hand, Workers are more independent and, above all, are systematically expatriated to African territories. It's the only way to see something other than one's place of birth, and to be able to combine the lifetime salary of a sedentary worker with the salary offered by the private company that employs her.

Friedrich groans and throws his hands up in the air. "What the hell are we doing here, in the middle of a war that does not concern us? I came here to make a bit more money, but certainly not to rot and maybe even die here."

"I can't believe you're still so naive," says Mallence shaking her head like an old cuckoo clock at mid day "haven't you ever wondered why the industry has been relocated to Africa?"

"There you go again with your theory. It was the banks, wasn't it that relocated them to Africa? Is that it?"

"Perfectly right," Mallence continues. "Don't you see that industries are the last to be able to fight against the tentacular power of finance and to have enough economic influence to counterbalance their power? In fact, since the 20th century, each crisis has enabled banks to buy up more bankrupt companies. If the biggest ones still exist, it's because their products are still indispensable. Have you ever wondered why we're in Africa rather than elsewhere?"

"Are you playing dumb, or what?" retorts Friedrich. "It's simply the continent of the poorest countries. Despite humanitarian aid, governments haven't been able to honor their country's debt, which they've had to sell off in whole or in part. You'll probably come up with something else," adds Friedrich, timidly sarcastic.

"The poorest countries?" repeats Mallence, imitating her colleague's voice. "I know there are clashes almost every day, but you've been out of the factory once in a while, haven't you? You've seen the country like me. You've seen the wealth extracted from the soil like I have.

Once Mallence is going, there's no stopping her, so Friedrich doesn't even try to answer the question.

"Plants producing zinc, copper, coal, phosphate, potassium, lead, nickel…"

"It's okay, it's okay," Friedrich admits, "I get it, it's true, there are plenty of raw materials here."

"See," says Mallence, "There's everything the Cartels need, even oil refineries, and I'm not even talking about diamonds and gold." Mallence pauses, as if to spare her audience.

"I've even heard that in Sierra Leone, some lucky people only have to dig in their own backyard to find some… If you ask me, it's the Cartels who needed help from African countries."

"And how do you think something like that could have happened?" asks Friedrich, still a little shaken by the originality of the analysis, even though he's heard it a thousand times before.

"Always in the same way, repeat for the thousand times, systematically destabilizing the political balance of the richest African countries and developing an image of chaos and extreme poverty among the sedentary population. This is why I don't really believe in the fate that's currently befalling us. It's easy to overemphasize the humanitarian aid campaigns of charities and make a continent teeming with wealth look like the poorest, most moribund place on the planet, surviving only thanks to generous help, when one owns the majority of the official news channels. And while they give on one side, smiling for the cameras, they plunder in the shadows." Mallence takes a moment and is almost amused by what she's about to say.

"You know that money isn't worth anything anymore, right? Since its gold equivalence was no longer honored, obviously, it would have been impossible to create the life wage if parity with gold had been maintained. There aren't enough gold mines in the world to finance such a project.

"Aah, you see," resumes Friedrich. "It's not all bad; it's been an extraordinary step forward this lifetime salary."

Mallence smiled.

"Well, come on," she continues. "Above all, it's a good way of keeping the few left, if any, who are still conscious, in check by making them fear the loss of their status. Don't forget that without a job, you're on the street, so everyone hides, everyone keeps quiet, because no one wants to become homeless. Besides, I wonder what all these sedentary people are doing, cooped up in their state-owned apartments. I wonder, but I have no desire to find out for myself. Boy, you've really made me lose my train of thought."

"You were talking about the value of currencies," says Friedrich, who is now completely depressed and prefers to return to the previous conversation rather than go on about the financing of the living wage.

Mallence pauses briefly and continues the tirade.

"Ah yes, the Cartel's currencies are worthless, and yet that's what they use in exchange for the gold and diamonds of *poor* African countries. If these countries had been healthy, wealthy and at peace, they would never have agreed to squander their resources so systematically and for such derisory compensation. So war had to be declared at all costs. It's the most lucrative and expedient solution. In fact, if I'd realized this earlier, I'd probably have applied for a job in the defense industry they're sure to have plenty of work." She continues her reflection in silence, then repeats aloud, "For all we know, they've even found a way not to have their production delayed by clashes. In any case, what happened in Africa will happen again. I don't know how, but I'm sure of it."

No sooner had Mallence finished her sentence than the siren signaling the end of hostilities, and the resumption of work echoed through the laboratory corridors. Friedrich blew out a breath of relief not to have to add anything to his colleague's appalling monologue.

It's pure paranoia, he thinks, *but how does she keep from going mad with all these Machiavellian ideas and plots she lends to our leaders?*

The resumption of the search is therefore carried out in the heavy silence of introspection.

Friedrich and Mallence are seeking to develop somatic cell nuclear transfer cloning techniques, in which the nucleus of an adult cell is inserted into an enucleated oocyte and the resulting egg is matured. This maturation, and the finalization of the cloned individual, have been greatly accelerated since the initial successes of 1996. Today, the sperm bank is able to obtain an operational being in less than a week. The counterpart of this accelerated maturation is that the existence of the synthetic individual thus obtained is capped at four hours. This is a real boon for the companies that use them, since they don't need to be fed, they just need to be replaced. Unfortunately, it's the recycling of these clones that has become a problem, requiring further research. Mallence and Friedrich's project is to double or even triple the life expectancy of the Cartels' sedentary populations. They also want to increase the nutritional value of the royal jelly distributed to these populations in order to combat the endemic anemia that weakens them and compromises social equilibrium. At least, that's what their contracts state.

Mallence carries out her contract work with uncommon seriousness and motivation, just like the model employee she wants to be in the eyes of her hierarchy, despite the doubts that keep her awake at night. No one, however, not even Friedrich knows that, during her many sleepless nights, she pursues her own parallel research. It's extremely easy when you're working all day on human cloning to put aside some of the essential raw materials without anyone suspecting a thing. So there's no reason to check the video recordings of his laboratory activities. Mallence wants to go beyond the life expectancy of the Homo convertibilis. She dreams of using it as a vehicle for human consciousness. She would like to be able to transfer consciousness from one clone to another. In a way, she's working on immortality, and no one must know.

At the same time, a meeting of the O.P.E.P (Organization of Private Entities of Production) was taking place in the conference room of the Gabon arms factories, Africa

In the conference room, a very private meeting is taking place. It is important enough for all the business leaders of the war-torn continent to have joined. Traffic in Africa is very difficult and extremely dangerous, so everyone is participating from a distance, but no one would have wanted to miss out.

The Commander of the African Revolutionary Armed Forces has also been invited. He is the only person physically in the room, enthroned in the middle of a huge empty room, seated on a chair worthy of a ministry and surrounded by control screens on which the company directors appear. Even the CEO of the arms factory where the meeting is taking place has connected via videoconference rather than joining in person.

He's been leading the African Revolutionary Armed Forces UBUNTU since the continent's first privatizations, and never have those little white guys stuck in Western suits agreed to provide logistical and financial support to revolutionary troops, without demanding actions that serve their own interests. Up until now, he had met with no one officially, simply receiving instructions from the Cartels when it came to sabotaging equipment in OPEP factories, or from OPEP when it came to organizing attacks in the Cartels. Things have now changed to the extent that he has been invited by OPEP. In person, he does not foresee anything good for the balance of the planet, but perhaps he will be able to reap some benefits for Africa and his cause.

The Commander's English is rather broken, and he only became a leader by force of circumstance. When the West officially bought his country after invading it and plundering its wealth and people for centuries, he decided to stand up and say, "No." Some of his brothers followed him, and a few whites financed him, sometimes in one camp, sometimes in another. Later, he realized that those who financed him were often as vile as those he confronted, but the reasons why these white-collar workers did something as incoherent as plotting against each other didn't concern him.

The meeting begins, and he watches all these puppets debate seriously and vehemently, hanging on the walls in their respective frames, like so many works of art on display at an unlikely exhibition dedicated to human stupidity.

One of the *paintings* speaks, "Before I begin this videoconference, I would like to thank the Commander of the African Revolutionary Armed Forces, on behalf of the OPEP, for his protection and support."

"It's funny to hear about protection from men who's armed all the wars in Africa," says the Commander, who refrains from smiling, even inwardly.

"We're on borrowed time, continues the *painting*. "*The financial powers that relocated us to this continent against our will run the cartels, while their governments organize the economic crises that are weakening us.* In the long term, they could even make us disappear."

"*International finance versus multinational production,*" laughs the military leader. "*In this area, I'll be happy to lend them a hand.*"

His expression gives nothing away; he remains cold and inexpressive.

Another *painting* takes the floor.

"Sedentary people live in hell, from birth to death. Under the guise of security, they are deprived of their freedom and the meaning of life. They die slowly, mired in boredom. We are the only ones to offer them a decent alternative. As manufacturers and employers, we can congratulate ourselves on offering freedom and a decent wage to as many people as possible. Yet the Cartels" policy of media intoxication has manipulated opinion against us, making a mockery of insignificant pollution problems. The members of the Investors Foundation succeeded in compromising us, isolating us on this sacrificed continent under the guise of ecology. It was not, of course, about protecting the environment, but about a ruthless economic war between international monetary exchanges, on the one hand, and our production force on the other.

One thing's for sure, the Commander thinks*, my African brothers aren't part of the greater good which these birds of prey are gargling at the moment. There are the powerful little whites, those they employ and the subhumanity they dispose of according to their needs, whatever their color and culture.*

It is to extricate his people and his continent from this state of affairs that he has vowed to fight to the bitter end.

"We're the force that's going to bring the big Cartels and their financial forces to heel, and we'll do it in the name of freedom," surmises a third *painting*.

The room fills with polite crackles of virtual, unconvincing applause, and one control screen after another fades out.

The screen, in which the factory CEO inhabits, remains lit alone.

"Commander," he said in a solemn tone. "We can't just sit back and do nothing. As expatriates in a weak position, we must take the initiative if we are to have any chance of emerging victorious from this tug-of-war with the Investors Foundation and the Cartels' puppet governments.

The soldier remains silent. The CEO continues, "Allow me to share with you some news that, until now, has been kept secret: the Sperm Bank laboratories in the privatized territories of Africa have succeeded in modifying SUBs so that they will soon have doubled cognitive capacity and autonomy. Homo convertibilis is going to be a reality that will revolutionize sedentary society as a whole and their work in the Cartels to the point of rendering them, in time, absolutely obsolete and useless. It will, however, have another, less official function. This should enable our industries to regain their place at the heart of Cartel activities and on their territories. By replacing the sedentary people in their work, Homo convertibilis will be able to infiltrate the sites of the financial markets and communicate this information to us. This will enable us to win the war of influence, which is at the root of our ostracization. If, by any chance, those who run the financial world of the Cartels discover what we plan to do thanks to Homo convertibilis, I wouldn't put much stock in the future of your continent. As for the alternative, which would be to provide them with the fruits of this research, it offers nothing better for the future of our industries and your people. We'd become obsolete and ultimately useless once the autonomy of Homo convertibilis reaches the decade mark.

After a long moment of silence, the Commander rises and, with an accent that would have forced good humor in other circumstances, declares, "Gimme the means, and you'll see that the response from the African States will live up to your expectations."

2078

Ubuntu had never really been able to achieve effective international terrorism due to a lack of resources. Above all, the technological capabilities of the intelligence services of the three Cartels of the 21st century exceeded anything the African Revolutionary Armed Forces could dream of possessing. Initially, terrorist explosives were almost instantly discovered and defused before they were detonated, and the soldiers sent to Cartel soil were intercepted at the border, incarcerated and tortured. The information that the intelligence services invariably managed to obtain in these cases was always extremely damaging to the African resistance organization. It found itself weakened and sometimes temporarily dismantled for several months at a time. For this reason, the Commander had even decided to confine his soldiers to local military operations on reluctant Cartel factories, preferring virtual terrorism when it came to international actions. This policy never prevented the media owned by the investors' foundation from flooding Big Brother with false information about the involvement of revolutionary forces in the explosion of a building or the disappearance of a politician.

When it comes to war propaganda, Nucleus has always known that it's essential to keep in the minds of the masses the idea of an absolute, evil enemy, uniquely responsible for the state of war, whose abominable actions jeopardize the sacred foundations of society's great social advances. He is convinced that war propaganda is extremely unifying, neutralizing and often imprisoning all opposition.

The revolutionary forces thus became true experts in cyberterrorism. Despite all this computer know-how, it was almost as impossible to penetrate the Cartels' computer firewalls as it was to carry out operations in the field. The commander therefore decided to attack their cryogenic system. Indeed, the energy expended in creating WVU requires constant cooling of the computer hardware, using powerful parallel circuits that are far less protected. After years of futile attempts, African hacker troops finally managed to hide malicious software throughout the computer systems of these cooling circuits, creating hacker-controlled networks ready to be corrupted at the opportune moment. OPEP has just provided that opportune moment.

Translated from Swahili:

"Keep a close eye on what all those little white OPEP scientists are up to, right down to the last details of the design of the new Homo convertibilis prototypes," continued the commander, instructing his troops on what to do when they gained access to the laboratories. "Send me even rough plans of the places you're going to discover. I don't trust these white-collar vultures who want to use us to regain some of their past power, and I want to be ready if we have to go on the offensive. I know that at the first opportunity, they'll make us pay for our success. Maybe they even want to use our operation to kill two birds with one stone, by ruining the Cartel's economy and getting rid of the *dirty negroes* who are sure to cut them off once they've regained their influence."

In the laboratories, production of the new SUB models, the Homo convertibilis, is in full swing. The first phase of Mallence and Friedrich's work has been crowned with success, and the autonomy of the new clones has increased from four hours to eight. This is still a long way from the weeks of autonomy needed to envisage getting rid of a new social category of sedentary people and soldiers in the armies of freedom, but this advance is still very promising. Neither scientist is supposed to be in this wing of the laboratories, which is entirely devoted to production, but Friedrich can't help hanging around here as often as possible. The presence of the terrorists they've fought so often within the fortress walls doesn't suit him well at all. Especially since the board of directors has apparently given them access to the design process and even allowed them to alter a few classified details to enable them to carry out their terrorist plans against the Cartels. Friedrich is out of his mind and finds the project insane, especially since Mallence doesn't give a damn.

How can she not care, seeing conspiracies everywhere? thinks Friedrich. *And in a few weeks time, our two hundred copies will come to term. I find it exciting, and she doesn't give in the least. We're really not made out of the same clay.*

But where is she, by the way?

As expected, the three Cartels bought the specimens before they were even conceived. Of the two hundred copies, one hundred are going to the United Americas, with the Grand Orient and Europe sharing the rest equally. To test their durability and efficiency, the Cartels planned to employ them in elaborate administrative maintenance tasks. They would also have liked to assign them to military affairs, but their autonomy is still too limited to allow them to reach the level of expertise required for combat.

Organized in squares and spread out inches perfect, the Homo convertibilis, their eyes in the haze, patiently await the moment of their embarkation to their respective continents. At this stage of their existence, they are not yet autonomous or *officially* born; they are, as it were, on standby. In this state, they consume only a tiny fraction of the non-renewable energy allocated to their conception. Once emptied of this energy, a SUB is unusable and must be recycled.

Mallence and Friedrich had once thought of feeding them by photosynthesis. Unfortunately, the energy absorption was far too low compared to the energy required for their metabolism, so that their withdrawal time was only delayed by a few minutes. Once on board, intercontinental supersonic flights will facilitate delivery in a matter of hours. These few minutes loss of vital energy will have no real impact on the tests carried out in the Cartels.

When the Homo convertibilis prototypes reached the European Central Bank in the financial megalopolis of Frankfurt, the representatives of the investors' foundation on site only managed to maintain their apparent nonchalance with great difficulty. Would the new models be up to the task? Would it be possible to further reduce the number of sedentary workers needed to keep the system running? Clearly, the Central Bank's managers have no wish to reduce operating costs, since their salaries are assured, come what may, by their financial activity and the fictitious creation of fiat currency. Their real problem is that not all the sedentary employees of central banks can work remotely, especially those whose responsibility it is to maintain the hardware of computer systems. The members of the executive wish to avoid, above all, a situation which could cause sedentary workers to become aware of their situation and risk a rallying of their forces motivated by desperation. The possibility is more than improbable, given the numerous reforms to the education system, freed from parental interaction, but it does exist and must, in time, be reduced to nothing. This is yet another significant step toward the obsolescence of the sedentary lifestyle and the increasingly absolute hegemony of the ruling caste.

Their first few hours in service lived up to their wildest expectations. The Homo convertibilis performed their duties like true sedentary specialists without any training. They did it before the eyes of the actual sedentary people. The latter did not yet realize that they were the direct witnesses of their own obsolescence. The UBUNTU technicians who had been authorized by OPEP to modify the prototypes could not risk equipping the Homo convertibilis with communications systems. They would have been intercepted in the first few seconds of transmission. Consequently, it was the cooling system's computer bugs that they evolved to enable them to detect a series of pre-established maintenance maneuvers operated by the new-generation clones selected for maintenance. Once spotted by the digital bugs, like a vault combination, the technicians know for sure that the SUBs are in place, ready to play their part, and that they can initiate the operation with certainty.

It's time for the Homo convertibilis clones to start the process.

The malware is immediately activated, and the cooling system stops working almost instantly. A few seconds later, an alarm informs the sedentary IT supervisors of the malfunction. They, of course, work remotely and can only pass on the information to the maintenance staff, whose function has been temporarily delegated to the new SUB models. The temperature continues to rise steadily throughout the computer network, while information continues to flow between heat detectors at the central bank and remote computers. The sedentary staff have no control over the network, and the sedentary maintenance staff have no initiative to join forces to neutralize the SUBs and regain control, nor do they know who to warn of the impending danger. The temperature continues to rise in terrifying silence and inaction. The metal cases that serve as hardware structures begin to melt, and the whole system decomposes in total ignorance and without anyone really caring. The synthetic beings had indeed been slightly modified by UBUNTU engineers. They had been fitted with a self-destruct protocol combined with a powerful explosive charge. It would have been discovered during the most cursory inspection, but who would have thought of inspecting SUBs? The supply of four-hour SUBs has always required a constant, just-in-time flow, making it technically impossible to control each individual unit.

One of the sedentary maintenance staff is standing right in front of the Homo concertibilis who was responsible for initiating the procedure. He could have sworn he saw the outline of a smile when the SUB whispered the final countdown, echoed monotonously by all the clones present:

"five, four, three, two, one." He doesn't have time to think about it any further when the whole building and a large part of the neighborhood disintegrate into molten metal vapor. That day, so will all the central banks of the three Cartels.

The Commander can be proud of the success of a state-of-the-art field operation.

Speech[iv] by the President of the Cartel of Europe, following the attacks claimed by UBUNTU and perpetrated against the Central Banks of the three Cartels, broadcast on all the Big Brothers of the free world

"Mr. President, members of the government, my dear sedentary people, On September 11, a terrible anniversary, the enemies of freedom once again committed an act of war against our Cartel of Nations. The Busers attacked our population, this latest attack directly targets our economy, and the night that followed fell on a very different world, a world where freedom itself is once again being called into question.

"Who attacked our Cartel?" asks our sedentary citizens.

From what we've been able to gather on the subject, everything points to the terrorist association "Ubuntu" and "OPEP," whose headquarters are in Africa. Ubuntu is to terror what the Mafia once was to crime. Its aim is not to make money, but to reshape the world and impose its radical views on the people of the planet. The leaders of this unscrupulous continent are linked to multiple Jouvencer organizations in over sixty States-Regions around the world, and finance the training camps that initiate future Busers into the tactics of sex terror. The fanatics are then sent back to their respective countries, where they hide out and organize their destructive orgies. Africans who don't subscribe to this radical vision are brutalized, and many die of starvation. Women have no access to education, and anyone can be imprisoned for no real reason. We respect the people of Africa—after all, aren't we economically attached to that continent, since the decentralization of our private industries, don't we have brothers or sisters working there? Aren't we the main providers of humanitarian aid to the native population? Our enemies are not all those African citizens, black or white, who have gone to work over there to support our economy and try to make a fortune. Our enemy hides in every leader and every government that supports this terrorist network, which hates what they can see of our constituent and legislative assemblies and elected governments. They hate our freedoms: those that have allowed us to question even the existence of God. They follow the paths blazed before them by fascism, Nazism, communism and all forms of totalitarianism. They will follow this direction to the end, where the unmarked graves of all past lie.

"How are we going to fight and win?" our sedentary inhabitants are still asking themselves.

We will commit all our means to defeating and destroying the terrorist plots of these illegitimate nations. Everyone will have to choose: to be with us or with the terrorists. From now on, any nation that continues to welcome and support terrorism will be considered hostile by our Cartel. We will take the initiative and coordinate an international strategy with our partners to guard against all forms of terrorism. Be prepared, I have summoned the private armed forces of freedom, and not without reason.

The time has come for our democracies to act, and we will be proud to do so. It's a question of world freedom. It is the fight of all those who believe in progress, pluralism, tolerance and freedom. We are grateful for the unconditional support we have already received from numerous regional states and international associations, such as the Investors Foundation. The free and civilized world is rallying to our side. It understands that without a unilateral fight, their own cities and people will be the next victims.

Our fellow citizens are asking, "What is expected of us?"

We ask them to live their lives. We know that many sedentary people are scared tonight. We ask them to remain calm and resolute, even if the threat is ongoing. We ask them to hold high the values of our democracy. None of them should be ostracized or mistreated in deed or word because of their race or skin color. Let's not pick the wrong targets. We are going to strengthen our economy and continue our efforts to reintegrate the homeless, in the name of the solidarity that characterizes any progressive society. We will not lose hope, we will not weaken, we will not fail. I hope that in the next few months and years, life will return to an almost normal cycle. We will return to our past lives and their routines. This is a good thing. Even the greatest sorrows fade with time. Our resolutions, on the other hand, will not fade. Each of us will remember what happened today and who was the victim. We'll remember when the news broke about our MMCs, where we were and what we were doing.

The outcome of this conflict is uncertain, but the benefits are certain.

Freedom and fear, justice and cruelty have always been at war. My dear sedentary people, we will defeat blind violence with impartial justice, convinced of the rightness of our cause and confident in the victory to come."

2080

Mallence has joined Ubuntu. There's often a limit to a person's ability to use cynicism to endure injustice and horror. Joining the resistance forces was the only way for her to stay sane. The commander decided to seize the opportunity and be the one to kill two birds with one stone.

The entire region's troops have gathered and hidden away in the jungle facing the laboratory's western gate. Everything is ready for the assault, as so often in the past, the difference being that Mallence has shared security weaknesses with the liberation armies. Combined with recent visits by UBUNTU engineers to the sperm bank's laboratories, the African officers have regained some optimism. According to her, the operators of the heavy weapon on the roof of the building, which has so far claimed so many victims, must prevent their shots from reaching the communications tower. It stands between the shooter and his targets in case of a Western attack. The shooter has to be very careful and aim precisely, which should give the besiegers enough time to break through the line of barbed wire protecting the laboratory and reach the door, whose codes they now know. However, nobody really trusts Mallence, but the situation is inextricable, and the choice was to take a chance and risk death fighting, rather than do nothing and die dispossessed.

The warriors of the first wave all know that they will not make it. Their sacrifice will allow the following waves to determine the angle from which they can penetrate without too much risk. One by one, the bullets hit, literally dislocating the bodies of the unfortunates in their path. The victims thus distributed on either side of the field occupied by the communication tower gradually form the strategic map of victory, toward which all the survivors of the following waves will rush. On the roof, Friedrich is in charge of the counterattack. He swears and rages at Mallence, whose absence has just been officially revealed, and who is undoubtedly behind this terrifyingly effective stratagem. He considered her his friend and she had always been his colleague. He also admired her intelligence and beauty—how could he not have seen this coming?

The weapon is too heavy to be disengaged from its metal axle by just one man, so Friedrich shouts to anyone who will listen, and summons the lab assistants to join him armed before it's too late.

Mallence does not take part in the assault. She is bound and gagged in a cellar near the fortress, ready to be executed by the Ubuntu warriors if her information turns out to be a trap.

Within minutes, the resistance forces had cut through the barbed wire, reached and unlocked the western gate and entered the laboratory compound.

Inside, the few members of staff who had not responded to Friedrich's call and were therefore neither armed nor on the roof, released the working SUBs to be used as camouflage and shields. The invaders are absolutely unleashed, exhilarated by their success and drunk with adrenalin; they've been trying to seize this emblematic Cartel fortress for so long, and now they're finally here, in force, to make their demands heard and recognize their identity. The haggard clones wander aimlessly through the corridors. They greet besiegers and besieged alike, promising to "serve them forever," until one of the many stray bullets interrupts their short existence and good intentions. Within minutes and without any real resistance from the staff, who are mostly scientists with little training in the art of warfare, the fortress laboratory is in the hands of the Ubuntu forces.

Meanwhile, in New York, the members of the United Nations General Assembly are completely uninterested in the outcome of this local conflict. On the other hand, in the wake of the attacks, the Security Council convened a meeting of the Executive Committee, made up of the three Cartel presidents and their three generals, at the headquarters of the Department of Peacekeepers.

It was unanimously decided to implement a retaliatory military operation against Ubuntu. The aim is to rid the planet of this terrorist vermin and their OPEP allies, who are "endangering the global economic balance and universal peace." In the high-security basement, the high-ranking dignitaries and officers meticulously spell out their own codes on the dials of their control screens. Following the procedure they have rehearsed over and over again from their respective continents; each inserts the key into the compartment assigned to them.

With the last turn of the sixth key, the process is set into motion, irreversible. While some of them have been dreading this moment since their first day in office, most are delighted and proud to be making history in this way.

In Africa, Friedrich and the few courageous lab assistants on the roof with him are petrified. After having endured, incredulous and powerless, an infernal racket on the lower floor, the details of which they didn't dare imagine, the silence and then the shouts of victory that follow indicate without a shade of a doubt the outcome of the battle and their imminent death. Defeated and resigned, they threw their weapons down the stairs to the roof, hoping to save their lives. The unmistakable sound of metal on the steps attracts the Ubuntu warriors, determined to finish their macabre business and take no prisoners. When all belligerents meet on the roof, eyes full of fear or hatred, no words are exchanged. Somehow, time is running out. The sky is suddenly darkened by a myriad of missiles spewing hellfire in trails of lava and sulfur. Decreasing-frequency whistles, so characteristic of bombing, rip through the equatorial sound spectrum and freeze their blood. Everyone looks up at the sky, almost instinctively, but there's nothing left to see but the inescapable horror of the next few seconds, and the hope that things will soon be over.

Today, almost the entire African continent has been wiped off the face of the earth. In the name of freedom, right, and justice.

"Finally! Hi Lextra," exclaims Laetitia, who appears to Electra J. on her phone screen like a devil out of a box.

"Hi, Laetitia, "Electra J. replies, struggling to shake off her daydreams.

"Can you open the door? What are you doing?" she continues, overexcited. "I've been ringing your doorbell and sending you texts for three hours. Are you avoiding me? I was starting to get worried."

"Sorry, Titi-San," replies Electra J., "until you called, I thought I was revising for my exams, but now that you've mentioned it, I think I might have dozed off."

Electra J. unlocks the door to the family home, and her friend enters the vestibule, full of barely digested teenage hysteria.

"Into my arms, my sleeper. I, too, have just woken up from a bad dream: my handsome Jérôme wouldn't marry me anymore and I'd end up an old maid in this residence. But here I am, wide awake, and I have no intention of wasting my last week of bachelorhood watching the hours tick by. You're coming with me tonight to the Video Rave 3D broadcast from Moscow."

"No, it doesn't really ring a bell," replies Electra J. without taking the time to think about it.

"You're a real party pooper," Laetitia laments. "I'm telling you, come on, it'll piss your dad off and we'll have a laugh, everyone will be there."

"And that's exactly what upsets me. We're going to see beautiful Slavs shaking their hips and giving us lascivious glances on the screens. Unfortunately, what we'll be left with in our living rooms, and to put in our beds, are the same old clean little faces with bodies sculpted with anabolic steroids, who we've been rubbing shoulders with since childhood. We know them by heart, they know us by heart because they've banged us at least once on the nights of great dearth, and I never want to have anything to do with them again. I don't want to live in a cocoon anymore, but I don't want to do it just to piss off my father either. I dream of being able to live for myself. I dream of being able to show what I'm capable of apart from him. I dream of being able to escape from this golden prison that reminds me at every moment of whom I'm the daughter of without ever giving me the slightest latitude. I don't want to end up like Christ, a pale copy of his sire who is only tolerated because of his family tree."

"Come on! You're not starting a depression episode, are you? First of all, you're really hard on your brother, but I think he's adorable, not to mention a great fuck"

"Please stop talking to me about it," Electra J. interrupts, her nose wrinkled in disgust, "you know the idea of you sleeping with him disgusts me and it's rather inappropriate for a future Mrs. Jérôme. I'd rather hear more about him."

The question that really burns Electra J.'s lips is, *By the way, remind me why you're getting married again?*

But she can't go on playing this acerbic role of the jaded or frustrated. She knows why she is getting married. She's getting married because her father asked her to. Jérôme is no worse than anyone else and has one very great quality: he's destined to go and live in one of the Grand Orient's Eden residences in Moscow as soon as he finishes his studies, to represent the bank his father runs. Ever since she was old enough to fantasize, Laeticia has talked of nothing but Slavs. The idea of finally being able to taste what she defines as "the very essence of eroticism" weighs, quite unfairly for Jérôme, enormously in the balance.

That evening, despite her reservations, Electra J. goes to the party. She is constantly reminded of everything she wishes she could forget—her father, the reality of the world beyond the walls of her gilded prison, the superficiality of her condition where everything is framed, codified and checked. She's read somewhere that the name Eden is a nod to past religions, representing paradise on earth for some believers.

Her father is the incarnation of a terrifying, vengeful god who reduces to nothing anyone who stands in his way or questions his decisions.

Submerged by these dark thoughts, Electra J. throws herself on the sideboard and sponges off one of the cocktail bowls until she reaches the point where things become less concrete, and problems are put off until tomorrow. She finally slumps onto one of the sofas facing the holographic screen and lets herself be carried away by the whirlwind that envelops her every time she closes her eyes. She casts a casual eye over what's happening on the screen.

"It's true that a Slav is beautiful," she said to herself, as she gently moistened her alcohol-dried lips, not realizing that she'd just spoken her thoughts aloud.

Beside her, as it should be, a clean-cut anabolized, freshly groomed and clean-shaven Edenian, scans Electra J.'s anatomy at retina-splitting photo quality speed. Admittedly, she's got a knack for dressing up from nothing. Her outfit consists of a small coral cotton tank top, very close to the body, enveloping her firm, well-shaped breasts without even revealing them in a provocative neckline. Her toned, pale legs are accentuated by an ingenious little white skirt, smooth and light, interrupting its modest function mid-thigh and leaving the surrounding male population at the gates of voyeur paradise. This sofa neighbor, unable to stand it any longer, thrusts out a warm hand, surprisingly dry, given the surrounding effervescence and rambling, inspired by the testosterone-fueled events projected far and wide from the great East.

Electra J., her eyes still closed, lets herself be surprised and convinces herself, from the alcoholic haze from which she is limply struggling, that this is one of the side effects of 3D projection. So she enthusiastically welcomes this unexpected foreign body, whose subtle touch expertly lavishes increasingly indecent caresses that carry her, in waves of pleasure, to the great depths of the oceans of bliss. The inquisitor's hand soon reaches the borders of the hymen, having slipped, without encountering the slightest resistance, beneath the ultimate intimate garment that symbolically protects the outskirts of her femininity.

Electra J. trembles with excitement, her back arches helplessly, and the new position further opens the lips of her overflowing flower. The finger spreads the petals and slides into the lair of a thousand ecstasies. Electra J., at the height of her desire, lets out a moan of pleasure that electronic music piously covers.

"Excuse me, Sis, I'm sorry to interrupt such a happy occasion, but Dad asked me to take you home and you know how much I hate disappointing him."

Electra J. doesn't need to open her eyes to realize whose hand it was that was giving her pleasure and the horror of the situation. As if driven by hatred itself, bloodshot eyes, she springs from the depths of the sofa and hurls herself at Christ, who fails to react soon enough to ward off this radical change of situation. In a matter of seconds, she lacerated his face and hit him with all her might and ends up pouring all her freshly ingested cocktail consumption onto his handsome suit. Immediately after, she loses consciousness as if she'd used up all the energy she'd accumulated during the coital preliminaries in those few moments.

Since the speech by the general of the international private armies, the implementation of the new patriot laws and the attempted eradication of the African continent, the government has been systematically persecuting busers. just like junkies don't mind using used needles, Winston spends his clandestine nights under bridges and in dark cul-de-sacs, licking the vulvas offered to him or smashing their little circle with the serenity of a death row inmate, just like junkies don't mind using used needles.

The grime that sticks to his skin every morning when he re-enters his lodgings is so resistant to water that he sometimes has to take up to three long showers to get rid of the last of the dark stains, slimy patches on his body and the odors of grease mixed with those of semen and urine in which they roll until dawn. In the blissful routine of his administrative work, Winston wonders about his new motivations. He feels invaded by an increasingly urgent sense of morbidity, even as, paradoxically, his sexual experiences open up stammering but encouraging social prospects. The awakening to a less dull social life pulls him inexorably toward his doom, between depression and the beginnings of consciousness. It's all so confusing. Nothing in his upbringing had prepared him for a rethink of this magnitude, but he regrets nothing, for everything is better than the dilapidated state he found himself in before his youthful life.

He recalls the previous day's encounters. Apart from him, one man and one woman stubbornly survive their lovemaking: Julia and Emmanuel. Winston knows all about the stamina of their bodies, having tested them on several occasions. Emmanuel has stamina that could have gotten the better of him many a time. As for Julia, her knowledge of the art of fucking makes her the undisputed leader of serial killers, ahead of Belle Guness and Elisabeth Bathory—she is said to have single-handedly exhausted nearly three hundred lovers to death.

Winston is also part of this new elite of busers whose bodies refuse to die. He's had to resign himself; he's going to have to live; he's going to have to find another way, a meaning to his life. Perhaps Jouvence is just a stepping stone to something even more important. Winston is thinking of leaving town. It's an unheard-of decision for someone who has never known anything but the four walls of his apartments since birth. Yet he takes it lightly, almost without thinking about it.

If I'm going to live, he thinks, *I might as well do it for something worthwhile.*

A barely sketched thought that represents little more than a vague feeling, an emotion more than a reflection, since "worthwhile" is a vague and radically new concept for him. Perhaps he simply wishes to escape this new form of routine that leads him every evening to wade through the urban mire, smearing dehumanized humanity with his sex.

No one knows what goes on beyond the borders of the sprawling cities. No one really knows where they end up, since no one dares go outside. Here's another thing that puzzles Winston: according to the media and legislators, the air outside is highly toxic and sedentary people should not venture outside more than twice a year… Winston has been spending his nights on the streets for months now. Apart from the infectious smell that penetrates him with every breath and to which he has finally become accustomed, the air doesn't seem to have poisoned him yet.

Tonight, as he leaves his apartment, nothing is really planned, and in the haze of his thoughts, Winston mechanically heads for one of the meeting points established the night before. They're different every night. No communication during the day is possible, since the state of emergency was declared, because, in the name of security, all sedentary people are under constant surveillance. Information broadcast on Big Brothers regularly mentions this "in order to fight effectively against this new form of sexual terrorism which is decimating our populations."

How did the original busers, who started out as heroic citizens putting their bodies at the service of science, turn into proven, hunted terrorists whose misdeeds, Big Brother echoes day after day? Winston can't explain it. Sometimes he doubts his own intentions, so eloquent are the documents provided by the journalists.

Humanity has never been so alone.

The rendezvous is a long way from Winston's home, and tonight's walk doesn't tempt him. Even the prospect of new bodies leaves him unsatisfied. By the time he arrives in the vicinity, it's past midnight.

He turns into the street and heads for the chosen cul-de-sac of the night. Suddenly, a group of mostly naked busers rushes toward him.

"We've been burned," yells one of them. "The delivery person were waiting for us to do us in."

Delivery men using their guns? Winston can't believe it, for him it's a first. Yet he hears gunshots, and they're getting closer. Breaking through his astonishment, he too starts running. There are a dozen of them, running like rabbits doped up on Jouvence or its counterfeits. When you can have sex and ejaculate multiple times a night, nothing will scare you, even if it is rather unpleasant for a man and even a bit painful to run with your sex blowing in the wind. Fortunately for Winston, he didn't have time to undress. Without looking back, almost without thinking, at a prodigiously high and sustained pace for people with no real training, the group finally managed to outrun their attackers. Yet the race goes on. No words are exchanged, the group moves in close ranks, going straight ahead in a once again silent darkness.

After hours of non-stop running, the landscape gradually changes; the buildings become less dense, the streets more and more overgrown with mud until they disappear completely. The busers won't stop their mad race until the early hours of the morning.

When the sun finally breaks through the thick layer of cloud that has concealed it since sunrise, the exhausted Winston discovers a new kind of desert[v].

In the beginning, trees were sacrificed to make way for ever more numerous and ever less solid dwellings. Then, those that remained in the countryside were eradicated to make way for ever more crops for ever more people, or to feed the ever-increasing numbers of livestock on which humans fed.

As more and more were needed, and more and more profits were to be made, farms became bigger and bigger, and more and more automated. Crops always needed more chemicals to protect them from ever more resistant pests.

Like radiation treatment of cancer in the 20th century, chemical treatments destroyed both beneficial and non-beneficial organisms, leaving the earth devoid of living substances.

Clinical cleanliness.

To be generous, however, the earth needs rot, mold and all those little creatures to aerate it through tiny galleries. Without these galleries, which make it porous, rainwater can no longer penetrate and water it. The earth eventually dries out under torrents of rain made acidic by a multitude of mistreatment, and the water, sliding over the arid earth, takes with it its last hopes of fertility.

The earth had gradually taken on the appearance of concrete.

For the fugitives, the situation is more than precarious; some of them are completely naked, and no one has any drinking water or food. After such a race, they are absolutely dehydrated, exhausted, starving and totally lost in this hostile environment. Their only chance of survival is to keep moving forward, hoping to find what they need to survive along the way. No one has spoken a word since they left town. There are no words to describe their experience or their helplessness. Nothing has prepared them for such an ordeal.

Little by little, suspicious glances are exchanged, and the group falls apart. None of them has ever been with sedentary people for anything other than the enjoyment of their bodies, and never after daybreak; this sudden precariousness plunges them into a terrible sense of paranoia.

The more the hours pass, the more their minds and bodies are tortured. Dehydrated by the sun and the race, starving, terrorized, lost in the middle of the rural desert with no chance of returning to their sedentary lives, with all the consequences that this entails, each fugitive sees in his companions of misfortune his informer or even his executioner; the hell so often spoken of during their studies and in the media had never been so palpable. The nudity of some further amplifies, if possible, the feeling of weakness and vulnerability. They try desperately to hide their bodies with their meager hands, and these vain efforts further illustrate the ridiculousness of their condition. The general distrust, of course, is unfounded. Everyone is far too preoccupied with their own survival to think of anything else.

Their tongues swell with thirst, their skin dries out and cracks under the blazing sun, and hunger makes them lose all sense of reality. Finally, the molecules of Jouvence become scarce in their metabolism, leading the addicts, each at their own pace, but irrevocably, toward a state of withdrawal and the abyssal depths of despair and panic.

Fortunately, it's easy to get your bearings in this vast, flat deserted environment, and eventually they spot a dwelling that's taller and less ruined than the others, taunting them from a distance that seems to grow longer as they advance toward it.

"I'm going to lie down in the shade of these ruins," stammers one of the busers, whose skin, so unaccustomed to the sun, is turning bright red without him really realizing it. When they manage to reach the remains of the old, detached house, they soon realize that this is not the salvation some had hoped for.

Although a semblance of a roof still covers much of the building, one of the walls has been almost completely knocked down, revealing a desolate interior. How long has this house been uninhabited? Winston can't remember ever having heard, even in his schoolbooks, of sedentary people living in individual houses since the great climatic and social changes. The group enters with a certain casualness motivated by the mad hope of finding something edible in these ruins of another time. The upper floors are inaccessible and, in any case, far too dangerously fragile to reach. In every room on the first floor, the same desolation strikes hard at the spirits of the fugitives. The resulting ceaseless disappointment digs ever deeper into their stomachs, the hole in which they finally agree to bury their thwarted hopes.

With their legs giving out, they slump against a wall or in the dust and ashes, provided they're relatively protected from the sun's rays. No one moves, and the deafening silence of this antechamber to hell invites fevered minds to inner delirium.

Then, with a concert of squeaks that rips through the overheated air, the outline of a trapdoor emerges from beneath the dust and rubble. It's Death itself that seems to emerge from underground to claim the souls of its victims. Eyes wide open, foam white and parched at the corners of their mouths, neither Winston nor his companions are able to realize that a stranger has just emerged from the dwelling's basement to assess and decide their fate.

The road

"Come on, buddy, they're all so messed up, there's no way they can hurt you."
As he finishes his sentence, the frail, innocent-looking head of a little boy emerges from the man's trapdoor.

His little boy.

The man still holds his revolver mechanically but is now more intrigued by these visitors and concerned about their health than his own safety. None of the sedentary escapees have moved. They may not even be aware of their new presence, but they're far too ill to really react.

"Dad, we have to do something, or they'll die, this one is covered in blisters and barely breathing."

"No, little one, that would be too dangerous, and please don't get too close to them. We don't know where they come from or who they are. Imagine if they finally came after us once they'd recovered."

The little boy pauses, looking annoyed, and continues pensively,

"I thought we were the good guys; that we weren't like all those people we run away from and who want to hurt us."

The man remains silent. He's in better health than these unfortunates, but he's no less weak and ill, and he doesn't have enough ammunition left to defend his child against so many people, should he be attacked.

Confident and patient, the child waits for the end of his father's reflections, convinced that he will eventually make the right decision.

"I'll go and get some water, you're right, we can't let them die like that without doing anything, but it's out of the question to let them get into the cellar," he whispers in his ear.

The man disappears again and returns almost immediately with a few pieces of cloth too small to wear, but sufficient to protect his son from indecent nudity, and some of the drinks stored in the cellar. No water, of course—it's too precious to share—but a few cans of soda.

He doesn't like leaving his son alone and unsupervised, and no sooner had he arrived in the cellar than he immediately regrets having gone down there without asking him to follow. This little being is his reason for living, his strength. Without him, he'd probably already be dead, swept away by despair.

As one sedentary person after another comes into contact with the drinks and the sugar they contain, they come to their senses and realize what's happening.

"Who are you?" asks one of them. "What are you doing here?"

"We've been living here for several weeks now, and before that it was more complicated," he says. "But for the moment, you're the one who's staying with us, and it's up to me to ask the questions."

Then, in the most threatening tone possible and brandishing his gun, he says, "And you'd better succeed in persuading me that you're telling the truth."

Despite the exhaustion in which they all find themselves, the sedentary people are stunned by what they discover in more ways than one.

First of all, the affection that seems to bind these two beings is absolutely unheard of and literally radiates. And then what are they doing alone, in the middle of the rural desert? They could only be homeless, yet this possibility seems unimaginable—homeless people can't just wander around. The man is undoubtedly the father of the youngest. How can this be? And he owns a gun, even though guns have long been banned from society.

"We've just come from the town, we were chased out of by a group of delivery person, so we can't go home at the moment," stammers one of the fugitives.

The child and the man look at each other as if they've just heard a foreign language spoken that they don't speak. After a long moment of silence, the father gently invites the child to bring back from the cellar some canned peaches, which they have in large quantities. This would have been nothing less than a fortune in a can for resourceful, sedentary Megalopolis dwellers ready to squander their treasure on "Ebuy." But for the runaways, at this moment, it's the very source of life, and they drink from it to the last drop of syrup.

Sugar dispels the last of the dizziness and Winston asks, "Do you have many more of these?"

The reaction is swift, and the man is immediately beside himself with menace. He brandishes his weapon, shouting as the believers of past centuries threatened the godless with God's wrath. Everyone quickly takes their rightful place, and the man realizes that he has nothing to fear from this band of weak, cowardly townsfolk. But he remains magnanimous.

"I'll give you a few cans of drinks and canned food, but I'm asking you to leave this house before nightfall," he says, glancing briefly at his son to make sure he has his approval.

"I don't know what your plans are," continues the man, "but you should know that a day's walk from here, there's a building full of people who look like you, where you can probably find better assistance. There's nothing more we can do for you here."

None of the Jouvencers have any specific plans.

"You seem attached to the little one?"

"He's my son," replies the man proudly.

Such a gulf separates the sedentary group from this unlikely duo that no one knows how to address the questions they all have.

"Have you met anyone else besides us?" asks a sedentary woman.

"Far too many," says the man, "and too often things have ended badly."

He pauses again.

"Whether alone and desperate, or hunting and surviving in groups, those we encountered were most of the time rabid, bloodthirsty beasts that had to be guarded against at all costs."

The world and society of men are so different from what sedentary people could have imagined.

No one is willing to say it clearly, not even to themselves. Yet this encounter, the magical relationship that binds man and son and literally fills the space where they are when they talk or simply look at each other, has shaken all their certainties. They, who are so suspicious, so aggressive at times and so cold toward each other, can't understand what could bring these two people together so tangibly and so strongly. Could it be the parental line?

They begin to understand that nothing that happens now is conceivable without the presence and help of others. Alone, they don't stand a chance; alone, they'd probably be dead already.

"We're going to rest a little longer, then head for that building that you told us about," concludes Winston, hoping to speak for the group.

No one will contradict him.

"I'm glad you agreed to meet me, sweetie, we've been seeing so little of each other lately, I had no choice but to summon you to my office." Nucleus pauses for a moment, knowing that he's not dealing with an ordinary interlocutor. This is his daughter, the apple of his eye. She possesses his cognitive power, his quick wit, his sense of timing, his creativity and his perseverance. It's for these reasons that he feels so close to her, and that the conflict between him and her so saddens him. But this is a delicate moment, and it's time to act with finesse.

"Let's slip away and have a coffee at the theater bar, shall we you'll probably be more comfortable there, isn't where you hold your little mobilization meetings?"

There's no need for him to add "against me"—Electra J. knows exactly what her father is up to.

It seems that he wants to put his cards on the table today... how do I go about it, play his game? Certainly not! thinks Electra J., who has been preparing for this interview ever since her father "begged" her to meet him.

She's sworn to herself not to get carried away; to ignore the tenacious admiration she's had for him since childhood, and which refuses to leave her. Every time she meets him, tears well up in her eyes almost automatically, and as soon as he opens his mouth and speaks to her, sadness immediately gives way to anger.

She immediately senses the tone of someone who wants to convince, to soften, sometimes to intimidate. She sees in his eyes the cold calculation behind the torrent of comforting but empty words he so skillfully lavishes. She's seen him do it with others too often to be fooled.

Unfortunately, she's weak and she knows it. Deep down, she'd like him to take her in his arms and hold her tight. She'd dream of feeling his love surround and protect her again, like when she was a little girl. She would dream of once again feeling the weight of her father's gaze weighing with pride and approval on her every action. She would dream of her father saying to her,

"I'm sorry, sweetie! I'm sorry for everything I've put you through since your accident. I'm sorry for everything I've done to bring the world to where it is now. I'm sorry for all the shenanigans and for all the lives I've sacrificed, I'm sorry for making you suffer so much when my intentions were completely the opposite. I love you, my darling, and it's this love that matters most to me, beyond power and money, beyond my own aspirations."

"Electra J, you're not listening to me, it seems," remarks Nucleus, interrupting his monologue and scrutinizing Electra J. to the very depths of her soul. She's petrified by the look she hates.

"Don't worry, Dad, I know your speech by heart anyway; I can easily miss a part... Where were you? Are you doing all this for my sake and yours? Or does the planet deserve to be separated from its poorest members so that it can regenerate? Or "Some sacrifices are inevitable when it's for the good of the many?""

"Please don't be so aggressive, Electra, I know you're suffering and I'm sorry, but I can't go on tolerating your attitude and your stances toward me; we're so much alike, how can you not see that and..."

Now Electra J. wants to cry and scream. Her whole body trembles with rage, fear and all those negative emotions she spends her days trying to control when she's away from her father. When she's in his presence, nothing helps.

"Father," she replies with all the dryness of her soul, then pulls her tone together and adds with flowers in her voice, "I'm very thirsty. Would you allow me to get a drink from the vending machine? Would you like me to get you something?"

She had to get away as quickly as possible to regain her composure. The conversation had taken the turn she'd been dreading, and she needs to regain control of her feelings. She had to talk to him like an adult and not like his temperamental, angry little daughter who had to be reasoned with or reprimanded. Otherwise, she knows, she'll have to live for weeks on end with the remorse and guilt of having lost her temper again, of not having done the right thing. Electra J. returns to the charge, two glasses of wine in hand and the firm intention of resisting any impulse. She's going to listen to him and not react. Of course, she's counting on the effect of the wine to help her a little. She calmly arrives at the table where Nucleus is waiting, places a glass in front of him and gently sits down at the table, her teeth clenched and her heart heavy, but a kind smile on her lips. The one she has so often seen lights up her father's face.

"Isn't it a little early for wine? You know, Christ told me about the incident at the virtual party."

Electra J. clenches her teeth even tighter to prevent herself from adding anything.

"I'm really very worried: you spend most of your time organizing meetings that harm me, and now you're drinking in public to the point of making yourself sick and losing all sense of dignity. Your brother didn't want to tell me anything, so I made him tell me the details when the story came to my ears. You know I always end up knowing everything."

"And he also told you what he did to me, I presume," she thinks, mad with rage, but her eyes are still impassive. Only her lower lip betrays her, trembling slightly. *You bet he didn't want to tell you. My poor Nucleus, you're as blind to your children as you are manipulative to the rest of humanity.*

"Talk to me, sweetie, you know how much I love you, if there's anything I can do to get you out of this downward spiral that's eating you alive and making me feel miserable. Help me to build a better world, help me to give meaning to all these sacrifices for which I am responsible in your eyes."

Once again, Electra J. feels that knot in her throat. She has to control herself, not give in to her emotions.

"Father, I'm sorry for what happened last time at the party and I can assure you it won't happen again."

For the good reason that I refuse to have any further contact with your son.

"As far as my position on your policies and actions is concerned however, nothing can change as long as I believe that your actions are dangerous and harmful to our future. I know you think you're doing the right thing, but it's never the place of one person to decide for everyone else. Even someone as brilliant as you. I know it, I feel it in my bones, and history has shown us time and again that power perverts, power drives mad, and we must guard against this madness. The first democrats wrote their constitutions in order to establish real checks and balances. Unfortunately, people like you have gradually modified these constitutions to their own advantage. As a result, the rest of mankind has forgotten their true usefulness, letting themselves be fooled by the few crumbs that have been conceded to them and the fine promises of a brighter tomorrow. If you're willing to consider this point of view, then perhaps working with you is conceivable. We could work to repair what's still possible. Otherwise, I'd prefer you to leave me alone or confront me if that's your choice. But above all, I'd prefer you never again to put the filiation that links us in my way.

At that moment, what Electra saw in her father's eyes was a staggering void of incomprehension and great sadness, but the knot that had blocked her throat for so long dissipated and her heart felt lighter. She had just lost her father, but for the first time she was able to be herself, in spite of him.

The next day is less arduous. At least the fugitive group has soda and enough food to last them until their destination. The dangers of turning up at the gates of a state institution, undoubtedly in constant contact with the megalopolis of Brussels, are not lost on anyone, but the situation is far too precarious for them to have any alternative. John's skin is covered in blisters, and any contact makes him scream in pain to the point of being impossible to move. So they had to build a makeshift stretcher and cover his body with the few scraps of cloth left to the group by the father and son.

They could have left him by the side of the road, but that would have been the death knell for the embryonic trust that is painstakingly building up between them. No one was willing to take such a risk.

At the end of the morning, they saw the shaky, uncertain outline of a building, silhouetted like a mirage on the horizon. In the late afternoon, they finally reach the gate. In the courtyard, a drinking water fountain. It's only thanks to a few vestiges of civility from collective memory that the busers don't kill each other at the sight of it. Probably also because the effects of Jouvence have completely worn off, and their poor physical health prevents them from becoming aggressive.

Greeting them on the doorstep was one of those four-hour lifespan SUBs. These manmade beings had cradled the childhood of each member of the group, without any of them really having taken the time to think about it. They had facilitated their birth and their upbringing. They all had the same features and the same name. There was something comforting about seeing them again in such desperate circumstances.

SUB takes the floor.

"Welcome, my friends. I had no warning of your arrival, but I'm delighted to be able to welcome you and escort you to your rooms."

The busers look at each other dumbfounded. A few moments before, they were about to enter hell, and now the gates of a little paradise were being opened to them.

The Weert rehabilitation center is already almost full, and Winston, Julia and Emmanuel have to share a room. The others are divided up according to availability, and none of them will be lucky enough to find a single room.

That morning, Emmanuel found himself admiring Julia showering. It's the first time he's experienced a feeling a little more elaborate than a primal desire. The water plays with her forms in a myriad of disorientated little torrents. He's not excited, he's tenderized.

It's been several days since the survivors moved into the rooms of their haven of peace. Every morning, a SUB brings them the day's ration of food, which resembles in every way the basic protein food distributed at discretion in each apartment, and everyone begins to settle in. Nights are calmer and more restful, and Jouvence's withdrawal is soon a thing of the past.

Seeing how comfortable the homeless are with each other and how much fun they seem to have socializing; Winston's group eventually communicates to the point where everyone knows each other's first names. Winston, Julia and Emmanuel are in a room. Bernard and Helmholtz have been forced by overcrowding to share a room, but they seem to have gotten on very well with it, since they still spend most of their day together. John and Lenina also share a room, but it has to be said that John's state of health requires the SUBs' full attention, and she'd rather wander the building's corridors than hear him moan.

Seriously sunburned during their cavalcade, he has since lost the epidermis over most of his body, and the lower layers are just as red and fragile. He has a high fever and hasn't left his room since they arrived.

In the early afternoon, everyone gathers under the dome of the indoor garden to enjoy the soft, filtered sunlight. Lenina finds it hard to understand why the homeless all seem so absorbed in their tablets.

"After eight weeks in residence, we take a competitive examination to determine whether we are fit to return to the city. If so, the government gives us a job, a house and a salary and we become sedentary." He says this with a touch of emphasis in his voice, as if for him, this is the pinnacle of professional achievement.

Lenina doesn't dare comment on what this homeless man has just shared with her. Of course, no one at the center knows who they really are. As far as everyone is concerned, they are homeless people who have come of their own free will. The little explanation improvised by the group at the time was enough to convince them, and no one asked them any more questions.

Lenina keeps her sedentary lifestyle and those of her companions to herself.

"If we fail," he continues, "it's the door and the desert all over again. Fortunately, thanks to the good treatment provided by the center, almost no one fails. You'll see, it's not very complicated, if you already have a few notions of reading, the rest comes very quickly."

"And for those who pass the exam, after how long does it take to leave the Weert center?" asks Lenina.

"As soon as possible," replies the homeless man, a little irritated at having to answer all these questions instead of studying. "Everyone's in far too much of a hurry to integrate into society to hang around unnecessarily, and then you have to make room for those who arrive. There aren't that many centers. The class is taken the next day to the lower level of the building, where the metro station connecting each center to the city is located."

Lenina's amazement is growing. Which metro is he talking about?

After a few improvised apologies as an epilogue, he gets rid of the ignoramus and Lenina has to leave him and join her makeshift comrades.

Just then, a SUB enters the room where everyone is gathered. He holds seven tablets in his hands. He hands one to each of them, explains in substance what everyone already knows, and nobody even thinks of interrupting him, so much so that the secret of their condition is more than ever to be kept.

So they set to work.

"The least we can say is that the level of expertise required for these studies is unlikely to worry the seven illegals. Nothing more than basic questions and concepts. Whatever function they're destined for, it certainly won't be too intellectual a job," Emmanuel quips.

If no one in the group trusted anyone yet, everyone could happily assess how far they had all progressed in the new art of communicating and making collegial decisions. In the end, the other was not quite as "infernal" as the Cartel of Nations slogan would have us believe, and the "infinity of their individuality" accommodated contact with others very well. If the calmness of the place was anything to go by, the other seemed to have many other functions than the one to which it had been reduced in the sedentary life of the past: giving and receiving pleasure in order to contribute to the productivity of the Cartels of Nations.

Nothing is the same anymore; Winston can feel it. The change came very gradually; to the point where it imposed itself on him without him even seeing it coming.

It has to be said that, definitively weaned on Jouvence, males learn modesty, sometimes failure at their expense, and have to discover new stratagems in order to achieve pleasant copulation. Winston didn't come to terms with this immediately, and on several occasions watched Emmanuel uncover Julia's body with his gentle, attentive hands. The first few times this even aroused his own desire, but the repetitions of these tender moments have brought Emmanuel and Julia so close that Winston hardly dares enter their bedroom to reach his own bed.

This new feeling of exclusion is very close to his image of psychological torture.

He overhears exchanges of glances that he no longer understands. There's something in their eyes other than desire, and he can't identify it. At first, Julia and the two men pursued their lovemaking in the grand tradition of busers, and then gradually their sexual encounters became spaced out and calmer. They softened.

Julia began to look at Emmanuel in a different, softer way. Winston even caught her blushing when Emmanuel's eyes met hers. Then the lovers locked themselves away and sought isolation. At first, they joked about having "locked" Winston out.

And then, when no one else laughed, Winston found himself alone again, and the suffering caused by this loneliness was even more terrible than before, because it was felt in the presence of others.

For their part, Bernard and Helmholtz have formed a cell so hermetically sealed that no one even thinks of talking to them; Lenina spends most of her time with homeless people, and Winston suspects her of wanting to betray the group. As for John, his increasingly severe and frequent asthma attacks and terrible bouts of hives have finally discouraged the SUBs from making any real attempt to treat him. Alone in his room, Winston can still hear him whimpering through the door between two expiratory wheezes. If he doesn't die before the first set of exams, he'll undoubtedly be expelled from the center the next time a homeless person arrives.

Winston is all alone, and the few moments of peace he enjoyed when he first arrived at the center are now only vague memories. On the other hand, the pangs of anxiety he feels at the thought of setting off again are very real. The center was never a sustainable option anyway.

However, between Lenina's comments, exchanges with the homeless and some discreet shadowing of clones, he knows where the spots reserved for the administration, from which the homeless are excluded, are; where the SUBs go to finish their service. Thanks to his studies, Winston knows all there is to know about the use and distribution of clones. However, he still ignores, no doubt in the name of the division of labor so dear to the society of great social advances, where and how they are designed and recycled.

It's also crossing this administrative zone that freshly graduated students join the metro on their way to the city and their new sedentary destiny. Food is no doubt also transported from the Megalopolis via this access, as no one ever reaches the center by crossing the rural desert. Everything seems to converge here.

This is where Winston intends to flee, and the sooner the better.

Winston had no trouble getting into the restricted area. There's no surveillance. No one ever intended to escape. Why leave a shelter that feeds, houses, educates and builds a future for the most disadvantaged? A place that promises a better tomorrow to those who have nothing, who are nothing, and whose condition is to die of cold and hunger.

As he passes the last empty offices, just before entering the corridors that run deep into the earth, Winston is overcome by a thought that imposes itself on him and chills his blood. The only members of society he knows or has ever met in his entire life are the sedentary, the delivery, the homeless and the SUBS. Here again, there's no one but the SUBs, who have very little autonomy, and no one to organize their replacements.

It's incredible that I've never seen a single shipment of SUB or even royal jelly, he thinks.

Everything seems to be fine-tuned without any visible supervision. Where are the sedentary in charge of the SUBs' work? What about those people he's admired all his life on his Big Brother; the actors, singers, TV hosts and politicians who unleash so many passions among the sedentary and who seem to live only in his multimedia complex? Do they really exist?

A gigantic cold sweat runs down his back like the shiver of a lie rolling down his epidermis.

"Of course they exist!" he exclaims, as if to rid himself of these parasitic thoughts by speaking louder than they do.

Despite this, he continues to reflect on the depth of his isolation as the escalator takes him deeper into the bowels of the rehabilitation center.

Around him, in the half-light of neon lights from another age, he discovers the remains of what was undoubtedly a tunnel system designed for human transport. The tiled, whitish walls exude a corrosive, ancestral mold, and the signs on the walls are barely legible. Yet, when Winston reaches the bottom of the metropolitan shaft, much more contemporary architecture and technology testify to a new use for the place that he can't yet grasp.

The lighting is different, more intense, but also warmer, and he perceives a gentle mechanical hum that curiously reassures him. Everything, from the colors to the shapes to the sounds of this new environment, is soothing. He heads toward the source of the hum without really thinking about it, and at the end of the corridor, just beyond the bend, he can already make out what he imagines to be a railway track.

It's hard to get a clear picture when you can only base your assumptions on photographic knowledge from history books. The smell has changed too. It's still pleasant, but his senses, alerted by the discovery and the risks to which he's exposed himself, indicate a kind of overkill of good smell. It reminds him of those air fresheners that supplant nauseating scents without making them disappear.

Winston hesitates. He's less afraid of being discovered than of what he's afraid to find out. The smell and the unease become more pressing. Forcing himself forward, he reaches the large cube in the center of the platform along the track, blocking his view of the other end. When he finally passes this blind spot, Winston contemplates a system of machines and containers, alongside which are lined up hundreds of human carcasses, hanging by their feet awaiting their turn to be packaged.

No homeless person has ever had the intention of escaping from a rehabilitation center, because that's where they're fed, housed and educated, and where their future is being built. Why put under surveillance a place that promises a better tomorrow to those who have nothing, who are nothing and whose condition is to die of cold and hunger? The homeless have no reason to worry about the intentions of those who shelter, feed and care for them, just as farmers once did with farm animals.

In his mind, horror mingles with disgust as, little by little, he realizes what's in front of him. First, he recognizes the SUBs, all of the same build, but others are also vying for the machine's gaping mouth. Many others.

He recognizes one face, then two. Some of the homeless from the previous class, those who haven't yet passed through the giant crusher of the packer, like the male chicks that traditional breeding got rid of for reasons of economy.

Winston suddenly realizes that for the first time, he's contemplating the great protein generator, considered by many to be one of the major discoveries behind the great social advances; one of those that supplies the sedentary dwellings of the Megalopolis with royal jelly.

Cold sweat runs down his back. He gets nauseous thinking about what he's eaten this morning and most mornings and lunch and dinner since he's been at the center. And before this fugitive life, when he lived only for his buser's evenings, how many times did he resolve to save on food to acquire the devices or pills that were to sculpt or wax his body, soften his skin and develop his power? And even before all that, at boarding school… For as long as he can remember, royal jelly has been his daily routine. Nothing really forced him to do it, it was simply more convenient and less expensive. For these reasons, and without realizing it, sedentary people have become anthropophagi. No matter how hard Winston dwells on what is staring him in the face, he is unable to fully embrace all the consequences of this discovery when he is interrupted.

The air fills with low frequencies and the platform shivers as a subway train appears. A score of SUBs get off, armed with their benevolent smiles and four hours of goodwill. The troop disappears almost immediately around a service door and, a few steps away from where he entered, Winston hears noises and a cheerful commotion. It's a new promotion leaving the center. A surge of adrenalin stimulates his instincts and refocuses all his attention on survival.

From a distance, he recognizes other homeless people, those who stay and wish the graduates all the happiness in the world; some are even still singing the traditional song: "Ashokan Farewell" from the depths of time as the doors close. The graduating class then heads for the metro train.

He'd like to intervene and warn them, but what matters most to him is escape. Leave this place, leave this sick society, but he doesn't want to risk getting caught again, only to be fattened up and end up as jelly on the plates of some Megalopolis' innocents. So he watches the funeral procession go by without opening his mouth, without flinching, in complicity. Yet he's so close, he can read the excitement mixed with a little fear in the eyes of some of the condemned.

Winston, shamefully concealed, has not moved to satisfy the unhealthy curiosity that prevents him from looking away, but the group can hardly make out the cold antechamber of the large generator from which they are standing. Even if they could, all their attention is focused on the subway train, whose neon lights illuminate the unlikely future of those already doomed.

As the last homeless man enters the wagon, the door slides silently into its closing position, and the latch sounds as it finishes its run.

Graduates expect to feel the oar start up, their leg muscles contract instinctively and their eyes search for a handhold.

None of this happens.

Instead of the expected racket, all they can hear is a light, steady murmur, like that of a Multimedia Complex switched on, but transmitting no program.

From his vantage point, Winston doesn't miss a thing of the show, especially as the vast majority of the car's walls are made of glass.

The blowing continued for a few more moments, then they all collapsed at the same time, as if synchronized to a fatal choreography. It was only at this point that the great din began. Concerto for springers, metal arms and automatic doors, transporting the group of graduates from the horizontal position on the ground to the vertical, suspended position of previous graduating classes.

A final automatic command, like the whistle of a sharp whip splitting the air, and the bodies of the victims begin a slow bleeding that ends up covering the metal floor of their shared hearse with a thick red tide.

Meanwhile, on the upper floor of the rehabilitation center, Julia re-enters the room and Emmanuel can't take his eyes off her[vi]. How could he have been so unaware all this time of the happiness he felt in the presence of his beloved? The light literally changed every time she was in a room. It was impossible to be better made, to have more lustrous, softer skin and more beautiful, better-shaped forms.

What eyes! What spirit!

Moved like a child discovering his first amorous sensations, Emmanuel moves gently toward the object of his desire.

And succumbing to the tenderest intoxication carries her to bed, devouring her with kisses.

His fingers tickle the buds of her breasts, and his tongue delves into the mouth of his precious. He soon realizes that these caresses act on his senses with inconceivable force, and he is overwhelmed by waves of bliss that make him dizzy. His whole body tenses toward the vulva, which he already imagines pink and shiny and divine to the taste.

"Wait," she said, on fire. "This time, let's take advantage of the moment, the happiness will only be greater."

At these words, she turns around and lies flat on her stomach, legs spread. Slipping his head between her thighs, Emmanuel devours her, admiring without restraint or modesty the rounded, firm shape of the most beautiful buttocks imaginable. In return, she gives with her fingers the same pleasures that her prince's tongue gives back. Emmanuel knows the gestures that torment his lover and intertwine his ardent tasting with forbidden caresses on the other border of her perineum. Intoxicated by this audacity and the effect it has on his beloved; Emmanuel devours the cum she spurts from her little cunt at every turn. Sometimes she interrupts her moaning to look at him, to observe his pleasure.

"How beautiful you are!" she told him in a breath, "oh, how good it is to feel your hands on my body."

Drunk with desire, testicles aching from waiting and caresses, Emmanuel replies, "I want my ram to finally knock on the door of your entrails and see you faint, intoxicated with my cum."

"Wait a little longer," she whispers, "I want to drive you crazy."

Julia now faces him, inserting two of her fingers into his sap-swollen flower without taking her eyes off him.

"Very well, my little angel, I'm going to offer you some more," says the lover, almost piqued.

His tongue immediately slips back inside her cunt. With one hand he teases her little circle and with the other he kneads her breast; thus receiving three pleasures at once, the happy girl convulses and the sweetest of sighs escapes from her mouth. Barely recovered, his mistress turns around, presenting him with her buttocks. Like a madman in crisis, he jerks off forcefully at the very edge of her ass. He finally takes it by storm, dilates it, possesses it, slams it again, victorious, and both end up, in a torrent of ecstasy, dying of pleasure.

He kisses her mouth, their tongues intertwining, tasting and sucking.

"Don't abandon my clitoris, my love, I think it's still strong," she orders, trembling, as she kisses her lover's still proud member. "Touch it tenderly, but don't scratch it; it's all electric."

Emmanuel is exhausted with love, but he wants to distill himself into cum for his queen and unload twenty times in a row if possible. What ecstasy. Each gives back a hundredfold what the other has lent, and it's impossible to work harder to give pleasure to the other.

It's impossible to find one that tastes better.

"Julia," he told her, "what I feel for you is something I never knew existed, and I want you to be mine forever."

"Oh, my love! Let my kisses prove it to you," she replies, tenderly caressing his now shyly erect member. "It's to you that I owe these new sensations; you've shaped my soul with your caresses, freed it from stupid prejudices and it's only through you that I finally exist in the world. In truth, you are infinity and hell was my solitude; I feel it; ah! How happy I am, if you feel it too."

"Yes," he replies, "I want us to finish dispelling these infamous sociopathic precepts that have so far troubled our lives? I want us to rediscover the elementary principles of nature and prove to the world that all the fables with which our minds have been fascinated are only designed to enslave us."

They look forward to a whole day of the sweetest voluptuous caresses they've promised each other. Unfortunately, it must be otherwise.

From the corridor, armed men in uniform enter their place of pilgrimage and without further ado kidnap them, taking great care to separate them for good.

These are not delivery person. Having followed them many times on his Big Brother, in reports on Africa, Emmanuel immediately recognizes the private soldiers of the Army of Freedom.

Hooded, gagged and contained in the inner garden, Emmanuel and Julia, otherwise completely naked, offer a deviant image of their recent intimacy, far removed from their new reality.

If the conversations are to be believed, Lenina, Bernard and Helmholtz have joined them, Winston is nowhere to be found, and John has died of allergies for lack of proper care. In fact, this is why the Freedom Troops have been alerted: no homeless person has ever suffered from allergies linked to pollution or the sun. Before the solidarity laws and the opening of rehabilitation centers, the homeless lived on the streets. Initially, many died from illnesses linked to the hostile environment. The others eventually adapted.

The Weert center is searched from top to bottom, while the homeless are confined to their rooms and SUBs are prematurely "withdrawn."

"Against all odds, it seems that the sedentary fugitive has discovered the underground maintenance shuttle and returned to town," reports one of the soldiers to his superior.

Winston reached his destination long before the Freedom Troops discovered his escape. He barely had time to let his mind return to the dreadful reality of his condition and that of his fellow human beings; the trip lasted only a few minutes. All he had to do was sit back in the cabin, and the shuttle was on its way.

At the terminus, the station is deserted.

It's a good thing because Winston, upset, exhausted and disgusted, is no longer ready to fight.

Continuing his wanderings, he slowly crosses deserted rooms and corridors, his footsteps echoing in these empty rooms and in his head like those of the tortured man being led to the scaffold.

After much hesitation and several wrong turns, Winston exits the building. On the pediment, he can read, engraved in marble, "Ministry of Welfare."

No one in the building. No one outside. There's a pungent smell of compost or mold in the air, the source of which is hard to determine, but which makes him terribly indisposed.

He walked slowly through the Ministry District, anxiously realizing that most of the windows of the sedentary dwellings were open or broken. Has horror pursued him this far? He chooses an entrance at random and discovers smashed apartment doors and curdled blood all over the walls and floors, but no bodies. Winston struggles to keep exploring.

Visiting the apartments, and despite his deep disgust at the surrounding scents, he salvages what can be eaten, provided it's not royal jelly.

"Where the hell is everybody?"

He tries several times to call out at random, first timidly, held back by an upbringing that sticks to him, then in full voice. No response.

He's the only one in this building, the only one in this neighborhood, maybe even the only one in this whole city. Returning to the street, he begins to realize the situation and hatches a plan:

I've got to get off the main arteries if I'm going to have any chance of meeting someone. He turns down the first perpendicular alley.

He doesn't know the area but having spent many nights and years in the dark corners of a city that repeats itself over and over again, he has no trouble finding what he didn't dare to look for. The further he advances, the more the already heavy, rich air releases putrid scents mingled with hints of fire perfumes.

"No way," he mutters.

At the bend in another alley, no doubt piled high above him by a crane or bulldozers, Winston discovers a gigantic human mass grave. Some bodies are completely charred, while others, less fortunate, are rotting in the open air. Nearby, the smell is absolutely unbearable, and Winston flees, terrified and struggling to catch his breath.

He soon realizes there's nowhere to run. The city is literally fermenting under similar mass graves, placed at random along his mad course.

After the attacks on the central banks and the attempted eradication of the African continent, the armed forces of freedom purged the megacities of the three Cartels one by one. They executed to the letter the final phase of Nucleus's plan to get rid of the weakest elements of the species in order to achieve the ultimate evolution toward the new order to which he aspires. This "demographic restructuring" was carried out without any mention in the media or on authorized websites, and consequently without the slightest suspicion on the part of any sedentary person, even when the executions were taking place just a few kilometers away. One by one, towns were emptied of their populations, to the ever-renewed terrified astonishment of the victims.

With each holocaust, in the other megacities, the sedentary killed boredom as best they could. They alienated themselves in front of their favorite program, spinning the hamster wheel on their treadmill, or risking their lives as outlaw busers in the dark alleys.

Meanwhile, the armies of freedom burned their fellow human beings after executing them to avoid any risk of an epidemic. The number of decomposing corpses is so great that it's unthinkable for him to stay, as the risk of contagion is too great. Even without any medical background, common sense and his sense of smell tell him to flee this urban cemetery as quickly as possible, especially as the horror is absolute. Winston discovers at his sanity's expense what compassion is. No crime could have merited such carnage, and on the faces that decomposition or flames have still partially spared, he can read the petrified expression of incomprehension.

Winston is alone again. Nowhere to go back, nowhere to go.

He is the Adam without Eve of a civilization that is no more.

Interrogations of terrorists are carried out at the Ministry of Communication. Since their arrest, Emmanuel, Julia, Lenina, Bernard and Helmholtz have spent most of their time in the stale air of their confinement hoods. Their oxygen-depleted brains have lost track of time, and their bodies are ankylosed.

In a monumental common bulkhead chamber, the inmates are suspended by harnesses from a system of rails, swaying like empty carcasses, unable to see, hear or even feel the presence of hundreds of others around them, sharing their fate. Occasionally and unexpectedly, a Ministry employee promptly interrupts their ramblings by ripping off the Velcro fastenings on the visors of their hoods, subjecting them to a lightning-fast questionnaire, which seems to them to have no logical sequence or interest: their name, age and date of termination of their sedentary contract, and other administrative questions whose answers the inquisitors undoubtedly know. Then the visor closes, amplifying the humiliating sway of their suspended bodies and barely giving them time to catch a breath of fresh air. After four weeks, the product injected into their veins produces the best results. Gradually, as one empties the drawers of a dead man's cabinet, every shred of memory disintegrates, every certainty erodes until even their names become foreign to them. This is when the Ministry of Communication's treatment really begins.

Julia and Emmanuel once again share a room, as do Bernard and Helmholtz. This is essential for verifying and confirming the success of the formatting: putting the opponents back into familiar situations so as to be able to deal with any reminiscences. Recalibration takes just 4 days, but the procedure is meticulous.

Day 1, Renaissance:

Julia and Emmanuel wake up in a hospital room empty of memories and in a state of advanced physical anemia. It's state zero. They look at each other like two dogs made of fine China, expressionless and emotionless, they have no memories, yet this state generates no anguish. Instead, they gradually come to appreciate the softness of the sheets that envelop them and the light that illuminates them. The distant sounds of bustling crowds reassure them. They don't speak; perhaps they can't even speak at this stage, but their senses are awake like two newborn babies opening their eyes for the first time.

Just then, Colonel Charrington enters the room. His attitude, however, is not that of a military officer, but rather that of a gentle, comforting father. He strokes their hands and hair and takes them in his arms. No words are exchanged, just human warmth. The Colonel is a master of the art of this exercise, and he manages to convey the love necessary for this first phase without needing to invest in the slightest sentiment. When he feels that the convalescents' emotional responses are adequate, with a wave of his hand, he invites the nurses into the room. Each receives two capsules of Jouvence. Their anemic bodies react almost immediately, and both groan with relief as the first hints of power wash over them.

Jouvence is definitely a molecule like no other! Thinks the Colonel as he leaves the room. He rarely has to go back. The rest of the day is spent relaxing the bodies of the convalescents, protected on either side by bed rails. They are delighted by succinct, but frequent and delicious meals, lazing about in short, repeated and controlled naps, which are combined with artificially induced lagophthalmos. This allows the trainer to continue recalibrating while the recruits sleep. For Julia, Emmanuel and the other future recruits, this is undoubtedly the happiest day of their lives.

The second day, Celebration:

When they wake up, the bed rails have disappeared. They are free to move about, and all the signs indicate that they have been invited to don the uniform that hangs prominently in front of them. In the room, an extraordinary breakfast awaits them, with ingredients they only know from books.

When a non-commissioned officer enters the room, with a determined stride and a frank smile, they still have no idea who they are or what function they occupy in this company. However, they're willing to do whatever it takes to maintain that place and identity. The headquarters is close enough to the hospital that the lack of communication required by command is not a cause for concern. The twenty recruits gathered for this short trip devote all their attention to playing the role suggested by the uniform they're wearing: straight eyes, rectilinear vertebrae and vectorial thoughts. Once they've disembarked from the military vehicle, other recruits await them, and the day will be devoted to them. It would appear that they are all "true heroes of the fight against terrorism, seriously wounded in action." The government intends to dedicate the day to honoring them and celebrating their courage.

Military parades, medal presentations and inspiring speeches interspersed the morning's program. At noon, in the common room, the meal is more frugal than in the morning. The conscripts don't say much to each other, but the proud looks on their faces speak louder than words: they count, they are important and recognized. Their lives have meaning. Isn't that all people can hope for in life?

Day Three, Exultation:

The recalibration continues on the night of the second day. After this very "military" day, devoted to social belonging and professional identity, the aim is to anchor the recruits' sense of dependence. They mustn't let a misplaced sense of morality make them renounce all the wonderful things that the army of freedom has to offer. The idea is to make them irremediably dependent, and what better way than with Jouvence and its marvelous side effects? The images induced during sleep are consequently more carnal and intimate in nature. They play with the most natural sexual impulses and combine them with certain much more cerebral perversions that sharpen them and increase their power tenfold. All night long, the recalibration brings the sleeping beauties to the brink of ecstasy without ever really reaching it.

By the morning of the third day, the newly acquired military rigor is barely able to contain the ardor of the Jouvencers. While no one in the hospital corridors dares broach this rather delicate subject with their roommates, everyone feeds off their still palpable dreams, the vision glorified by each other's desire.

At around seven o'clock, just after a breakfast that more closely resembles the previous day's military breakfast than the previous day's feast, everyone is summoned to the hospital's shared basement shower room for the obligatory shower. One of Nucleus's theories is that all you need to do is create the right conditions to trigger the hoped-for chain reaction, without having to invest any personal effort.

Under a cascade of artificial rain, the naked bodies of the recruits brush up against each other one too many times. The social dam holding back their inappropriate desires cracks and finally gives way. It's going to be a long day for these new athletes doped up on Jouvence, but by bedtime they'll have scoured, tasted and consumed every inch of their training companions' bodies. With their bodies satiated and their souls relieved, Emmanuel, Julia, Lenina, Bernard and Helmholtz and their brothers in arms are fully operational, mentally and physically.

On the fourth day, Colonel Charrington will have to train these hundreds of recruits in tracking and combat. As long as there are still sedentary people on the run in the desert countryside, the security of the new order is in danger of being compromised. The army of freedom needs fresh meat to maintain a lasting peace and carry out its mission of purification. The fact that its ranks are fed by those it is fighting against is a cynicism that delights Nucleus. His new order is definitely built on extremely solid foundations.

The Federation[vii]

Of the one hundred and twenty million Edenians who now make up the planet's official population, it goes without saying that none are sedentary or military, all have close ties to the Investors Foundation and very few were aware of the Nucleus project. Of those who did, none had the slightest idea of the scale of the social change and the horror of what it entailed. Until now, no one had been able to seriously envisage such global coordination, but that was without taking into account the new communication tools and cutting-edge technologies available to billionaires like Nucleus.

On the fourth day, when he makes his first virtual intervention on the intranet of the Eden residences of the three Cartels and addresses what he considers his people, they are all stunned by what he has to say.

"My friends, it's often striking for a man to ask himself what the main purpose of his life is. For some, it's the quest for a happy marriage, for others amassing a large fortune. Once this goal has been identified, everyone works toward it, with varying degrees of success, for the rest of their lives. I've also asked myself this question, and what immediately came to mind was the urgency of serving the interests of my planet for my descendants.

After drawing up a list of the various things we needed to do to achieve this, and the ways in which we could go about it, I became convinced that we were limiting the opportunities available to our children, and even worse, that we were only giving birth to half of what should be our descendants, because too many habitable territories were being monopolized to house the low breed, sedentary populations of our Cartels.

I am deeply convinced that we are representatives of a superior species, that of the victors, beyond all racial or cultural considerations, scattered throughout the world, and that the more numerous we are, the better the world will be. We need only look at the various parts of the planet inhabited by sedentary people, or at the overpopulated privatized territories of Africa, the scene of barbaric and bloody tribal conflicts, to consider with relief the alternative where we are in their place. I'm convinced that every parcel of land added to our territory allows our descendants to come into the world. Index more and more of our planet under our government and all conflict is abolished and the natural balance restored. The idea germinated in my mind and, as it grew, became a plan.

All over the world, there are members of the investors' foundation whose mission is to implement this utopia. These members and their children have been patiently selected, subsidized and educated over the centuries in our schools and universities by older members. They watched the young to discover who, among thousands, would have the intellectual strength and sensitivity, stamina, eloquence, perseverance or determination to merit joining the ranks of our organization. Our ultimate goal is the promotion of a single empire, that of the members of the investors' foundation.

It was already the theory of Edward Levingston Youmans and the dream of Cecil Rhodes almost two hundred years ago, and of many others since. The names and influences have changed, the rules and players have changed, but the objective has remained the same: that of a new world order in which the strongest prosper and the weakest disappear.

It was probable, it was possible in past centuries, but after an unprecedented ecological and social crisis, an economy restructured around financial investments and freed from production constraints, and the perverse and murderous uprising of the planet's sedentary Cartels, it had become an absolute necessity.

Make no mistake about what was really at stake with the sedentary uprising. It was nothing less than a revolution. A revolution whose outcome could only be the extinction of one of the antagonists, them or us. If, in the end, it was the mediocre, the lamentable who perished, it's only fair, since the safety of the inhabitants of Eden residences and that of our descendants is thus assured. With the extinction of the sedentary and the eradication of the privatized territories of Africa, a new society can finally be born. It is one in which we no longer have to worry about the laborious. It is a society freed from work, production, growth

140

and, consequently, pollution. With a global population of one hundred and twenty million and a production surplus initially planned for 12 billion people, we have resources, means and technology we don't know what to do with. We have so much space that we no longer know what to do with it. This gives us the time we need to shape a new social and political organization that will be the cornerstone of the society of our children and our children's children.

I can officially announce that we, the one hundred and twenty million people who once controlled the world's destiny, are now the only individuals allowed to set foot on its soil.

I proclaim this day the first of a new existence for each and every one of us. An existence where pollution, overpopulation and war will no longer exist. To mark this new era, we're going to rename our beautiful planet to draw a definitive line under the past.

Welcome to all those who believe in this new beginning. Welcome to the Edenians, the people of Eden, the blue planet."

2084

Decades before the Great Purification, in the most privileged circles of society, pregnancy gradually went out of fashion. Within a few generations, none of the Big Brother stars—be they political, economic, financial or from the world of entertainment—went through childbirth to give birth to their babies. Women of the 1% society, as they are dubbed by alarmists and conspiracy theorists, have preferred to use surrogate mothers to bring their embryos to term, with the help of highly qualified doctors, often from the same 1%.

The sedentary women who volunteered rented their wombs for up to ten years of their monthly salary. Even if they didn't know the identity of the parents, they could always try to guess it by cross-checking the information distilled by the mainstream media. What pride when one of them could claim to have carried the child of such and such a personality.

So everyone was satisfied.

Given the number of sedentary residents, it was never a problem to find a surrogate mother when an Eden family wanted to expand.

Electra J. also wants to have a child, but she doesn't want that child to have any genetic connection with her father. This is one of the many punishments she intends to inflict on him. She therefore wishes to acquire an egg whose genetic characteristics will be as close as possible to her conception of perfection.

She goes online to "Meltic," one of the medical-social networking sites set up for this purpose. She first fills in a very precise questionnaire, which enables the search engine to determine the type of egg and sperm it can offer the patient, based on her income, professional activity and hobbies. As far as Electra J. is concerned, there are, of course, no limits.

She then chooses the color of the eyes, the maximum possible height, intelligence and good health. Who wouldn't want the most beautiful, healthy and intelligent baby possible? At the time of finalizing the sale, no sperm batches or surrogate mothers are available. Unfortunately, the site is unable to meet this demand.

How could it be otherwise? The planet has been purified of all sedentary people by her father. If she wants to give birth to a child, she can't delegate gestation to anyone else.

Not her, nor any of Eden residents. Although a little apprehensive about the prospect of pregnancy, Electra J. is determined to see her project through to the end.

Surprised that she hadn't even been able to get the sperm samples she wanted, she decides to seek advice from her local gynecologist. She obtains an appointment two days later.

"Unfortunately, Electra J., the chances of carrying your baby to term are very slim," her doctor tells her a little too bluntly after running the necessary tests. "You're not the only one," he adds reassuringly.

What the doctor won't tell her is that very few of her patients manage to keep their embryos to term. Rare are the patients of colleagues from other residences or other Cartels. If recurrent miscarriages were caused by a virus, it would be the most virulent epidemic in human history. The vast majority of women are no longer able to carry an embryo, and the vast majority of men are hypofertile.

Doctors in every practice had been coming to the same conclusion for some time, given the gigantic collections organized by the sperm bank, but in view of the recent global humanitarian crisis, the fertility problems of the wealthiest women had not been considered a priority.

This dysfunction was made all the more pernicious by the fact that, until then, no one had bothered. Edenian women didn't want to bear their children, and the number of sedentary women willing to do so, though certainly also decreasing, was high enough to provide for their needs.

Much later, researchers would discover that the GMO foodstuffs that had become widespread during the 21st century, combined with the endocrine disruptors contained in the most common consumer products, had ended up inducing other genetic modifications in both women and men, making the majority of uteruses unsuitable for gestation, reducing sperm quality and increasing the risk of hypospadias and cryptorchidism in boys.

Now that the planet's population had been reduced by 99%, the reality that no one, not even Nucleus, had ever envisaged became clear to everyone.

The vast majority of Eden's population is unfit to procreate.

How long can a man walk, without food or water, without direction and without hope? Winston's legs now seem to have a will of their own. They continue to wobble and their owner to sink ever deeper into the rural desert. The more the days pass, the more desperate the landscape becomes. Most days, his feet sink ankle-deep into black swamps of arid soil and acidic water, unaffected by the sun's rays that eat away at his skin. His body is covered in blisters caused by acid corrosion and the powerful UV rays that the fragmented ozone layer barely filters out. All around him, almost as stubborn as he is, the corpses of a few trees seem to point their gaunt, burned tops toward the cause of their ordeal.

No other presence, no other sound than that of his footsteps tearing through the poisonous clay with disgusting sucking noises.

Not a soul in sight. He is all the more certain of this, as his field of vision presents no obstacle. Only a slight fog in the humidity-free air and the sweat beading from his eyebrows prevent him from seeing infinitely.

On his way out of town, Winston picked up an old bag and as many containers as he could find and filled them with water-cut royal jelly. Since then, despite his disgust, it's been his diet.

The makeshift bag that laced his shoulders at the start and taunted him with nonchalant lapping at his every step is now dangerously light and silent. No matter how much he rations himself, there are only a few days left before his meager reserves run out.

While his mind may look forward to the prospect with some morbid relief, his stomach, throat and tongue refuse to give up and let him know it painfully.

He stops and puts down his bag, which sinks slightly into the peat. The sun, despite its merciless efforts, failed to dry out the fetid matter, as if the water it contained was too heavy to evaporate.

Winston withdraws one of the last gourds, already dangerously empty, and allows himself two gulps of royal jelly, which he swallows with both disgust and relief. He cursed the survival instinct that forbade him to sit and wait for the end. He curses the unalterable resistance of his body, discovered since the first Jouvence take. He curses the society of men and those who shaped it, he curses this desolate land that can barely support his weight. He remains on his feet, holding his head high like a golf ball perched on its support, waiting with little faith for the expert, decisive strike of an unlikely golfer.

With an almost intimate whistle, a bullet from nowhere suddenly smashed into Winston's jaw, shattering it. He remains motionless for a moment, his eyes vague and his consciousness in suspense. He slumps gently and rests his bloodied head on his bag, as if finally allowing himself a little rest.

The truck carrying the soldiers of freedom takes an infinite time to reach Winston. Thus suspended above limbo, still alone, waiting for an end that never comes, despite his mouth that he can no longer close and the pool of blood that floods his throat, Winston is relieved; he no longer has to fight; someone has decided for him. His vision blurs. He hears something, conversations perhaps, but can no longer rely on his senses. He can't move his head. Above him, a shadow looms…

Julia.

Military reports are piling up from all the Cartel bases, reporting nothing but mass graves and isolated executions. Nowhere on the planet have the sedentary fugitives managed to get together and organize any kind of resistance. Too busy surviving in a hostile universe or killing each other out of fear or cowardice, they had succeeded in doing what Eden's leaders themselves feared they would fail to achieve: their total extinction.

In any case, the planet has reached a level of toxicity that makes survival in the wild almost impossible. The few who survive will eventually die of hunger, thirst or infection.

Eden, stripped of its excess humanity, is ready to rise from the ashes.

Well, not quite yet. There are still the troops of the armies of liberty, whose function is no longer relevant because of the lack of resistance. However, they remain potentially dangerous because they are armed and of inferior social stock. Since the reproduction and education of the sedentary masses no longer took place within the closed confines of the family unit, but within a more official framework of national or even international public salvation, the various governments had put in place a number of reforms aimed at controlling the few sedentary people elected by them to protect them.

From an early age, teenagers selected for their physical strength and docile character were removed from the conditioning centers and placed in military schools. The apprentice soldiers didn't go out much more than the sedentary apprentices; their computerized conditioning program was simply different. In order to compensate for any physical malfunctions and to be able to constantly track the position of troops in combat, the Cartel governments had authorized, without any real prior agreement from the individuals concerned, the implantation of a nanotechnology chip, called a "Vital Chip," in each new cadet. This provided online medical applications with infinitely accurate information on the state of health and position of each cadet throughout his or her tour of duty. This technological advance was then presented to the sedentary population as a major social advance, and the military as "courageous visionaries who were willing to lend their bodies to science in order to develop an infallible healthcare system." It's true that the results were immediately dazzling, and many soldiers were diagnosed, treated and cured of diseases that had previously been incurable. What has been less emphasized in the promotion of these little bugs is that computers can also send them information. The vital chips were placed on one of the small vessels that irrigate the brain. One of those which, unfortunately, sometimes swell and burst.

Emmanuel, Julia, Lenina and Helmholtz are truly happy. Military life has given them a close-knit community, a fulfilling profession and passions they never knew they had. Julia, for example, is now widely recognized as an exceptional sniper. Until a few months ago, she knew nothing about firearms, and now she can shoot a sedentary person at over two thousand meters with her service weapon and without a tripod. The whole brigade, including the officers, is impressed, and even though no one has ever paid her a single compliment, she can see in their eyes that she has become essential. As for Lenina, she has no equal when it comes to locating and tracking down sedentary terrorists. They form an unbeatable team and are inseparable in the field and under the sheets.

Today's hunt has taken them into the backwoods of the rural desert, where the sun beats down relentlessly on reflective peat soaked in heavy metals, liquids and pollutants that it refuses to dry up. The blindness caused by this reflection prevents most of the brigade from discerning the fugitives from the imperfections of the landscape; most, but not Lenina. Isolated on the small turret overlooking the "perpetual" VLRA, she scans the horizon for the slightest suspicious movement. Sedentary people often move in twos or threes. Very rarely more than three, as their lack of social sense quickly plunges them into a paranoid frenzy, and they often end up killing each other. On the other hand, Lenina had never met a single sedentary person, or at least never one alive. Yet she had no doubt that what she saw through her binoculars, at least two thousand meters away, was a sedentary man. He's obviously in very poor health and stumbling along. He's so slow that it took her longer than usual to locate him with any certainty.

"Hey, Jules," exclaims Lenina, directing her voice at the group of companions a little lower down.

"Have you spotted one of those party poopers?" asks Julia.

"I think so, come up and see, I think you'll shoot your load."

The joke is a bit heavy-handed, but in Lenina's defense, humor, like interpersonal skills, requires training and a certain predisposition, which she seems to be singularly lacking.

Julia, who doesn't have much more of a sense of humor than she does, laughs out loud as she climbs the turret, just in case…

Over two thousand meters, her binoculars confirm.

I'm going to need a tripod and a lot of luck.

Fortunately, there's no wind today. Julia takes her time adjusting the tripod and her weapon on it. The sedentary man is perfectly still anyway and seems to be looking for something in his backpack.

"This guy is a complete idiot. He stops completely in the open and without taking the slightest precaution. If I shoot him, it's really to do him a favor."

This remark is curiously a little funnier than the previous one, but, once again due to a lack of training, no one cracks a smile.

Julia inhales and exhales three times, as is her ritual. On the third exhale, she pulls the trigger.

The target immediately collapses, and a roar of contentment shakes the canvas protecting the troops from the sun's rays.

"I think I've had it with the buser!"

It takes a long time for the perpetual VLRA to reach the target. Julia climbs down from her turret and then from the truck, approaching the body of her victim. The blood is already dried by the sun, but Julia notices with surprise that the sedentary man's head is resting on the backpack, as if he had decided to take a little nap.

Your nap's going to be a bit longer than expected, my friend, she thinks, wishing she'd thought of this new line of humor out loud.

The sedentary man stares at her so hard she's almost embarrassed. She takes out her service weapon and points it at him but changes her mind; he seems to want to tell her something. She leans forward to hear better, stumbles and collapses, struck by lightning.

All Freedom Army troops on the planet are equipped with the "Vital Chip," and many have been saved by it in the field during the sedentary uprising. The armies of freedom are owned in one way or another by members of the Investors Foundation, and Nucleus, as president of the foundation and CEO of Orson & Orson, the planet's largest pharmaceutical company, has access to medical computers. His own ethics and the magnitude of the task he had set himself forbade him from taking charge of the final phase of the major clean-up, but he was given an account of it that leaves no room for doubt. The army, as usual in this guild, reacted as one, and all succumbed at the same time and without suffering, whatever their geographical location, from a lightning aneurysm.

All that's left to do is let the bodies rot and the weapons rust away so that the new world order can finally become a reality.

EDEN

2084 – PRESENT TIME

2084

"Today, Mom died. Or maybe yesterday, I don't know. No doubt she'd been dead a long time, only her obstinate heart still beating.

Nucleus perverted, manipulated and finally destroyed her. I hate my progenitor.

It's impossible for her to live alongside such a predator without losing her humanity. You can't share his choices and decisions without losing your soul.

I lost mine when I was eight years old in one of the magnificent rooms of my parents' home. I turned on the Big Brother that was there by mistake and should never have worked. I did it out of curiosity, or rather subborness. I was eight!

The image of the world I had unknowingly constructed, the one that had quietly sustained my reality, shattered before my eyes, in a bloodbath. In its place, the truth of existence appeared to me as cold and implacable as my father: a dead fauna and flora and a humanity enslaved, sacrificed in the altar of so-called higher interests.

Nucleus said to me.

"In the 20th century, millions of lives had to be sacrificed for India to become one of the greatest powers of the Great East Cartel."

For each modernization, how many shantytowns razed to the ground, families evicted, populations decimated by disease, children exploited and sacrificed?

How can you be happy when you know the price?

He also told me —

"What I'm doing, I'm doing because I love you and your brother more than anything, and I know that the planet is doomed if drastic measures aren't taken. These measures I am taking so that you can live in peace, happiness and opulence rather than famine, war and fear."

He used to say to me —

"Don't be weak, my daughter. In nature, it's always the strongest who win

153

and the weakest who disappear. We are the strongest; we must survive; it's our duty to perpetuate our species and it's my duty, since I have the power, to see to it that my people are spared."

How I hated him! I hated him for being so loud, for being so sure, when, since I was eight years old, I've lived in fear. I hated him when he managed to convince me without ever being able to dissipate the terrible knot in my throat.

It's time to stop being weak, indeed, to take my destiny into my own hands and live up to my deepest convictions: no one has the right to dispose of billions of people with anonymous impunity. I'll never be able to bring back to life those who perished or even undo what my father built on the ignorance, naivety and suffering of his fellow human beings. But I'll put all my strength into fighting against his vision.

Anonymity was one of the major forces that propelled the first phase of the Nucleus project to success. He knows, however, that for the final phase, he must step out of the shadows, introduce the new world order and establish himself as the architect and promoter of this gigantic enterprise. Such a challenge would intimidate any other man, especially as Nucleus's family is in disarray and his primary motivation was to protect them. His daughter refuses to see or even speak to him. He has no confidence in his son, Christopher, who, on the other hand, never leaves his side and spies on him to the point of being viscerally exasperated by his presence.

His relationship with his late wife had gradually deteriorated to the point where he hadn't consulted her in years, even though she'd been the first to be enthusiastic when he'd outlined the beginnings of what was to become Eden. Of course, the eradication of almost all humanity was not part of Nucleus's plan at the time. He smiles fondly as he recalls that she had even been the one to unknowingly introduce him to the concept. She had unearthed an obscure, never-edited manuscript, sent in 2024 by an obscure, never-published scribbler, entitled: "Practical Guide to an Atomic Democracy." The title had whetted her curiosity, and she had read it in one go. It was about a system of strict democracy, managed by ultra-secure banking-type software, AGORAPP, which allowed direct political commitment by citizens in the drafting of laws. Nucleus immediately sensed that he could use this idea to build his society, but there was no question of introducing this new political organization to the general public.

It would be kept for the exclusive use of the global elite, members of the investors' foundation, and would be introduced when they alone remained. He didn't want to risk a dangerous awakening of common consciousness that could have led to a powerful reform of the system, without violence or uprising, and a challenge to his own hegemony. He wanted violence, he hoped for uprisings, and he planned a revolution so he could finally rid the planet of the surplus of useless humans. He proposed to the chosen few, chosen by him, the ideal society he had gradually conceived around this reform of the political system. His first decision was to finance the creation of the software in the greatest secrecy, and to ensure that the author would never be published. This was easy, since he or his friends in the investors' foundation were the main shareholders in most publishing houses, large or small. After a few well-placed messages, the scribbler returned to his "extra-scribbling" activities and the literary world never heard from him again.

It was time for Nucleus to introduce the implementation of major social advances. Once this first phase had been successfully completed, the final phase of his project could finally be introduced to "the chosen ones." The implementation of the new order is more than a vision, it's a necessity.

The Edenians, scattered all over our planet, are the great winners of their societies. They are the champions of the old regime, the leaders or descendants of leaders of the previous oligarchy. They are fed on power and imbued with luxury; in each of them slumbers a despot. To ignore this would have been a fatal error. On the contrary, given these facts, we need a system that is nothing short of perfect, so that no one can seize power, and so that everyone can demand accountability from others. He has no desire to turn wolves into lambs. On the contrary, he wants the hierarchy of wolves to be known, recognized and respected, so that everyone can take their place and play a leading role when the time comes.

He also wants to gradually reintroduce the use of traditional seeds, which he keeps preciously in his safe, and to do everything in his power to rehabilitate the rural desert. Until such a balance is found, they plan to live on the stocks that were previously barely enough to feed twelve billion people. They are more than enough to comfortably provide for one hundred and twenty million Edenians without having to consume or produce anything. When this balance is found, he will completely and definitively desynchronize political power from financial power so that these external forces do not influence social forces to the detriment of Edenian society.

Today, Nucleus presented his business plan to the other members of the investors' foundation.

"Unfortunately, it was from this inaugural speech, I believe, that Edenians unilaterally hated my father. For very different reasons, it's true, but with a vigor whose authenticity they all share. Some hate it for what it has done to the rest of humanity. I think it's safe to say that Electra J., my sister, represents this group in the most active and effective way. Others, among his closest collaborators within the Investors Foundation, for the overly democratic stance he seems to want to take, and whose anachronistically "populist" purpose they fail to understand. Others because they have been excluded from the steering committee of the New World Order. Most, finally, because they want to take his place.

Yes, Daddy's all alone. For the moment, the element of surprise remains in his favor, and the organization he has set up, or rather inherited, is outstanding, but it won't be too long before all those detractors organize themselves into plotters. Old reflexes are hard to lose, and I don't want to be far away when the most virulent strikes.

And then there's the problem of fertility. You don't have to be an astute plotter to understand that this will very soon be the main subject of controversy and tension."

The son of Nucleus is actually called Christopher, but for as long as he can remember, people have always called him Christ. As a child, he was, according to those around him, so handsome and gentle; always smiling and polite. He always wore his hair long, and his ocher complexion, combined with a deep, dark gaze, never failed to inspire visitors to remark on the striking resemblance he bore to the thirteenth-century Christian icons collected by his father in one of the family salons.

It was also born at a time when the biblical "Christ," the Christian's one, was officially recognized as a myth. For these privileged ultras, it was perhaps also an unconscious way of mocking him by desecrating the name.

In spite of everything, Christ remains the son of Nucleus, undoubtedly the most powerful being on the planet and the determining factor in the destiny of his fellow human beings. In this sense, the diminutive was somewhat premonitory. The only blot on this flamboyant picture is his sister Electra J. More intelligent, more tenacious, more serious, she's everything he's not. Of course, his father never really compared the two of them.

"You've inherited your mother's sweetness," he used to tell Christopher as a child, stroking his hair when he was paying Electra J. his umpteenth compliment.

Even after Electra J.'s accident and the radical change in her attitude toward her father that followed her slow recovery, he suffered in silence, but only had eyes for her.

Now that she openly accuses him of crimes against humanity for organizing and perpetrating the genocide that led to the creation of Eden, he continues to ignore her attacks and defend her.

His sister's greatness makes him small. Every day, her attitude reminds him of his own limitations and his inability to make his father proud of him. Nucleus's admiration for his daughter makes him insignificant.

For all these reasons, he hates them.

He was young and inexperienced, and his hatred was incipient when he managed to repair the Big Brother in the family home that traumatized his talented sister.

Now he has more experience…

Although Edenians have always lived in self-sufficiency in their homes, the disappearance of the sedentary population means that nothing is as it was before.

The guardians no longer come. Purification was too extensive and systematic to have spared them. SUBs are no longer produced, since Africa has been wiped off the map, so they had to completely restructure the maintenance of the residences until they could find something better. The financial and political activities that kept the financial sharks away from their families and on their toes have become obsolete, and everyone finds themselves "confined" and idle in this gilded environment, creating unforeseen family tensions among Edenian families.

Eden residences have long been self-sufficient when it comes to food, but no one is there to organize distribution anymore. Here too, something has to be done. So many tasks that no one, really no one, is prepared to take on. Not even to organize. Not even to consider. And yet they have to be done. One more thing to add to the long list of grievances against Nucleus.

"Can you believe I'm forced to leave my twelve-year-old daughter's education to artificial intelligence? We don't have anyone to employ; it's the last straw! No more teachers, no more cleaning staff…" As Maria describes her situation to Serena, she realizes the extent of her disaster: "no more architects, no more developers, no more innovations since the destruction of Africa and the annihilation of all sedentary classes, no more new spaces to conquer, only Eden, this island of garden encircled by hell whose upkeep we can no longer even delegate. It makes me sick! And our men, who used to spend their days amassing more power and more wealth, are now forced to live on an equal footing; it's a real torment. It really is. Having to deal with these sharks non-stop, all week long, is becoming more and more unbearable. What used to be almost charming in small doses is no longer so. Besides, what's the point of being rich and powerful if everyone else is as rich and powerful as you? What's the point of not being cold or thirsty if no one else is?"

Serena can see that her friend is getting carried away, but seeing no way of contradicting her, she refrains from intervening.

"And then his crappy egalitarian system is driving our men hysterically mad with frustration and boredom." Maria is now red-faced with anger and only manages to catch her breath with great difficulty. If she could, she wouldn't hesitate to get rid of this tyrant and his whole family. She knows she's not the only one, but for the moment it's too early and Nucleus still has too much ascendancy and power to risk anything. For this, at least, Maria is patient, but for the rest; there is no longer a money market and what the use of extraordinary means when everyone has roughly the same resources and daily chores can't be passed on to anyone.

Maria went from anger to tears.

"We're heading straight for disaster! I never thought I'd have to say this, but I miss the sedentary people."

It's these small details that make the absence of the sedentary more tangible and disturbing. Their interactions with Edenians were almost non-existent, but everyone knew they were there. Their condition made Eden's happiness more tangible, without anyone really being aware of it. Of course, no one wanted them to suffer, just as in the days when meat was still edible and carnivores refused to find out what happened to animals before they reached their plates, for fear of spoiling their appetites, for fear of having to change their habits. In the face of a lifetime of suffering, abuse and torture, everyone blames those responsible.

For livestock, this meant farms and slaughterhouses.

For the sedentary, these were governments.

Moral is no better among men. Christ, always on the lookout for his father's criticism, for the latest grievances heard in the gym: financial trading revenues and the global economy are at a standstill. Even if the reasons are obvious and the situation temporary, the big capitalists in the residence can't wait any longer, moping around the gym or, worse still, at home. The last inter-residential videoconference went rather badly, and it would seem that tempers are no less frayed elsewhere. Criticism of Nucleus is less and less veiled, and the animosity toward the residence where he lives is, of course, increasingly ostentatious. Everywhere, beyond the protective bubbles of Eden residences, is the nothingness of cities invaded by the dust of bodies incinerated on site. It is the nothingness of deserted countryside drowned under the putrid sludge of industrial waste. It is the nothingness of acidified oceans, unfit for life. How ironic! Edenians reign as absolute masters in the deepest boredom on a dead planet, and their infertile bodies are the sad incarnation of this.

Electra J. is rigorous and very systematic. After hours of Internet research, she knows why things are going wrong. Even if everyone tries to ignore her, Electra J. isn't fooled.

We have to rebuild without repeating our mistakes. That's our duty. It's the only way to make sense of the billions of deaths. It's the only way to justify the fact that we're still alive, she believes.

The recent discovery of endometrial nidation problems makes the need for this timid resolution even more acute. Is her home the only place to be affected by this wave of endometrial hyperplasia and teratospermia her gynecologist told her about?

She needs certainty.

Thanks to the financial clout of their populations, Eden residences have had outstanding communications infrastructure since their creation. In each of the 170 countries that make up the world's three major cartels, just over a hundred residences have been developed. Each residence can accommodate up to 6,000 residents in conditions of luxury unimaginable for a sedentary lifestyle. They all work in partnership or competition, so communication is vital to the success of their business.

Given the scale of the task and the need for the utmost discretion, Electra J. succeeds relatively quickly in obtaining the information that's so important to her:

In the residences she has managed to contact, the medical conditions of the Edenians are identical. With an average of ten births per residence for the previous year, when by chance the lovers were compatible, future generations have a compromised future, to say the least.

A vile but understandable feeling of comfort invades Electra J. She's not alone, she's not cursed, what ails her is a global phenomenon.

She knows her father; she's seen him do it far too many times. He's not going to let anything slip, and he's going to set about solving the problem before it becomes too obvious to the Edenians and triggers a wave of anger that will be fatal to him.

Electra J. refuses to beg for information, refuses to be an accomplice to these schemes and, above all, refuses the possibility of working with him and becoming his accomplice. She wanted to take her future into her own hands—now's the time.

The solution must lie elsewhere. It can't be found at the bottom of a test tube or in the secret files of his progenitor's collaborators.

I'm leaving tomorrow, thinks Electra J., whose decision is ahead of her reflection.

When her conscience returns, she realizes that the undertaking is not so easy. Commercial aviation is totally grounded at the moment, so she won't be able to travel outside the Cartel. Especially as the pilot assigned to Nucleus has disappeared, along with all the other private military personnel seconded to the residence.

If she manages to cross the borders of her country, she'll be lucky. So she'll have to rely on the private car her father bought her when she came of age, which she's never really used.

Who would need a car when you have a driver, a pilot and even a navigator at your disposal to travel from one Eden residence to another? Thought Electra J. shamefully.

I'm no better than Nucleus. How could I have been so carefree and so lacking in an analytical mind as not to see the overflowing luxury in which we lived in comparison with the aridity of the landscape that unfolded as far as the eye could see, on the other side of the bubble? How could I have been so oblivious to the rest of mankind's need to adapt to this hostile environment that I never even gave it a second thought? All my childhood, my entourage, my tutors and my parents kept telling us that life outside the residence was dangerous, and I accepted this as a truth in its own right; a truth that was not to be discussed or questioned. A truth that was imperial for Edenians, but which excluded the rest of humanity. I thought I was intelligent, cultured and lively. I'm so ashamed.

It's not easy to pack a suitcase when you have so few ideas about the terms of travel. So Electra J. awkwardly piles up what she imagines to be essential. When her phone rings, she ignores it, fully committed to her project.

It's her brother.

The fact that he's trying to contact me bodes no good. Let's hope the car still works! She thinks as she closes the cellar door of the family home for the last time.

When she reaches the basement, it's not a car she discovers, but truly a car dealership. All, it seems, of the new generation of perpetual motion vehicles.

My father's demands for luxury can sometimes be of use... she muses, as she chooses the most spacious and best stocked with drinking water and protein.

What she notices immediately on entering is the great silence that reigns. No sound transgresses the glass boundaries of this mobile sanctuary. Not even when Electra J. electronically initiates the engine's perpetual motion. Not a sound. These are things you notice less in company. In solitude, silence is deafening.

She enters GPS coordinates outside the residence because she doesn't know how to use thought control.

"You have to start somewhere." She sighs.

The fully automatic car drives off obediently, taking with it what Nucleus loved above all else, with no desire to return.

Even if the roads between Eden residences had been maintained to facilitate business travel, it's true that these journeys had become less and less necessary. They were rarely made by car, as Edenians were too afraid of meeting the wrong people…

Electra J. can hardly believe what she sees.

Greenish sludge splashes across the horizon as far as the eye can see. The smells she imagines being fetid do not reach her, but the glass structure of the car offers a panoramic view of the horror that surrounds her luxurious skiff. Nature no longer has defined contours, and everything blends together like the decomposing flesh of a forgotten corpse. The car struggles to stay on course, so slippery and uneven is the asphalt, and there's no way of distinguishing when what used to be called vegetation ends and begins.

Electra J. sweats profusely, despite the air-conditioning; cold sweats of anxiety.

The extraordinary comfort of the vehicle no longer allows her to ignore the appalling hostility that reigns just a few inches from her, on the other side of the cabin. She could tint the windows or even make them opaque, since she doesn't need to drive, but the prospect of seeing nothing terrorizes her even more.

She could never have imagined such desolation.

Her courage and tenacity lose strength with each new kilometer. Nothing has prepared her for such an ordeal, neither her parents nor her studies. How far can she go before the environment overwhelms her fragile equipment? She's like a sailor in the middle of the ocean, preparing to weather a terrible storm. Unfortunately, while he can rely on his willpower, knowledge and experience, Electra J. is helpless and destitute if the vehicle comes to a standstill.

For the moment, it's moving along…

"You have arrived at your destination," announces the synthetic voice.

The GPS breaks the silence of her thoughts, the car comes to a halt and the engine stops.

Nothing and nobody moves.

Outside, not a wisp of wind. One might almost doubt the presence of air were it not for the computer's constant assessment of its quality. For the moment, it's 74% breathable, according to the computer.

"Big deal," exclaims Electra J., mimicking a conversation, "even if it were 110%, I wouldn't set foot outside."

Her inappropriately elegant outfit is smeared with perspiration. She sits upright, wide-eyed, on the unfolded berth of her luxurious vehicle, ready to wage a desperate battle against an intangible danger.

"Would you like me to open the door, or would you like to program a new destination?" asks the GPS.

Electra J. is caught off guard; where to go? However, she is quick to exclaim much louder than necessary: "New Destination," as she worries the computer might take the initiative and open the doors to her sanctuary.

"Which is the nearest Eden residence on this road?

"The nearest residence is Rotterdam, 213 kilometers away. Other possible destinations are…"

Electra J. interrupts.

"I would like to visit the Eden residence in Rotterdam."

"Very good," says the speaker immediately.

A slight electrical stimulation is felt, and the engine's perpetual motion resumes its infinite course.

2085:
Christ's letter to his father

Dad,

We're under attack from all sides. It's only been a year since the creation of Eden, and those we considered our partners are turning against us.

I've just heard that Electra J. has left the residence. Did you know?

Research is at a standstill, and although we have managed to reintroduce non-genetically modified seeds, it is still impossible to plant them in the ground, and cloned farm animals are so medicalized that they remain unfit for consumption. SUB production is still halted, and Edenians find the situation absolutely intolerable: their homes will soon be as filthy as the streets of the old sedentary cities. Air analyses seem to be getting worse and worse, both in the countryside and in residences, and we're seeing more and more deaths from respiratory failure.

Speaking of deaths, according to the latest census of the three Cartels, nearly ten million people have died this year. At this rate, and without a lasting solution, our population will be completely decimated in just over ten years' time. While these figures are in line with global statistics prior to the Great Purification, they are extremely worrisome given the insignificant number of births. The few mothers whose children have survived are now the guinea pigs in our laboratories, and this is feeding the ranks of our opponents.

For the time being, the water purification system are working properly, but I've personally spoken to one of the Edenians who has offered to monitor it, and he's very pessimistic. They're designed to work automatically, but in the event of a malfunction, and without a trained team, it will be impossible to prevent an interruption in distribution.

The implementation of direct democracy is going nowhere, because there are too many detractors, and each of them wants to use your failure as a springboard to power.

I've been indirectly contacted by several of your advisors who wish to reform a parallel oligarchic government that will take over if things get worse. Wolves don't like idleness, and they now have every opportunity to use their free time to our detriment.

Dad, I'll always be by your side, and you can count on my constant, loyal support, but I'm afraid we're becoming increasingly isolated and powerless.

Your son, who loves you.

Christ slips the freshly written letter into his father's still-warm hand. The glances they exchange at this moment are a mixture of incomprehension, sadness and hatred. Until this final moment, Christ had never admitted to himself just how much he hates Nucleus; not when he was plotting against him, not when he was preparing this macabre interview, not even when, on entering the room of his peacefully sleeping father, he intended for him the physical manifestation of his poisoned soul. From his earliest childhood, gnawed by a lack of recognition, then devastated by the death of his mother for which he blamed him, Christ has learned to let go of all remorse. His pain, rage and frustration has become his only fuel, driving him to act without conscience. He wanders in an emotional coma.

After a few brief jolts, Nucleus's body comes to a standstill, the mouth and eyes wide open as if to help life go away.

"This way, Dad, you won't say I didn't warn you," says Christ, placing the syringe on the floor next to him, from which a drop of the lethal liquid he's just injected is still beading.

Without the slightest expression or movement toward his father, he left the room.

169

On the day of Nucleus's burial, no one is fooled by the circumstances of his death.

A member of the audience mutters through gritted teeth, "Such a psychopath could never have taken his own life."

"It certainly wasn't the death of the sedentary population that weighed heavily on his conscience. And it wasn't a few complaints expressed by his vassals from other residences that could have worried him or called into question his hegemony," added one of the worldly gravediggers invited to the funeral ceremony.

It has to be said that Nucleus had done a good job of imposing its system of atomic democracy. The principle of direct democracy was absolutely remarkable, but, like any human construction, it has its weaknesses, which one needs to be aware of in order to negotiate them in everyone's interest. This was obviously not the case. To be implemented, atomic democracy needs to be managed by software, which, itself, needs to be managed by an administrator. In Bouquillard's project, the administrator was a group of three randomly selected citizens, supervising dedicated artificial intelligence and counseled by experts. Only Christ and a few others knew this detail, but in the Nucleus project, the only administrator was him. Or was. Now it's Christ.

Lose one, gain ten" thinks the crowd.

In a grave tone dictated by the circumstances, Christ speaks,

"Eminent Administrators, dear Edenians,

Nothing touches us more deeply than the death of a great leader. Nucleus Orson,

170

a great man, a remarkable leader, the friend of all democrats, an extraordinary father, the fervent defender of dignity, equity and justice, the apostle of peace, ended his life."

Nucleus was a white-collar vermin without conscience or scruples who successfully perpetrated the largest genocide in human history. Now he's the apostle of peace. An apostle who then usurped his power from the survivors of this massacre by passing himself off as the fervent defender of fairness, paraphrases in substance and thought, most of the audience whose silence Christ mistakes for emotion.

"What might drive a being to commit such acts?" continues the son of the deceased. "May never be known, but we do know that such acts are often motivated by the kind of doubt and extreme despair that seem to echo at the very heart of our new world."

"Or maybe the echo of this motivation resonates deep within the bottomless cavern that lies in the place of the heart of the one who helped him die," says one of the Edenians present, almost inaudibly.

"This one didn't die on the cross either," says another, triggering a river of coughing fits among those still trying to conceal their giggles.

"If we truly love our own, our planet and this new order offered to us all by my late father, Nucleus Orson, if we believe in justice and mercy, if we want, without restraint, to build a better world for generations to come, we owe it to ourselves to condemn without appeal the hatred that consumes individuals at the root of doubt and despair, the false accusations that divide us and the bitterness that turn us against each other."

"Or we can also decide to take back power!" This statement, as unexpected as it is inappropriate, rises anonymously from the heart of the assembly.

The silence deepens and Christ pretends not to have heard anything.

"I hope that the ultimate sacrifice of our beloved leader will soften the hearts of those who strive to spread venom and poison our minds.

"Our people are in mourning, the whole world is poor for what it has just lost, but we can all be better because Nucleus Orson has shown us the way. Now, free of the almost inhuman burden we had imposed on him, may he rest in peace."

After nearly eight hours on an impassable road, the car came to a standstill. It's hard to describe what Electra J. felt at that moment: a concoction of disappointment, dread and renunciation.

"Eight hours to cover less than two hundred and fifty kilometers. Trains used to do more in two hours nearly two centuries ago!"

Now that the car has come to a halt, it's only a matter of time before the headlights that currently illuminate the night fade, and with them all hope of a happy ending. Even if she's convinced that Rotterdam Eden has located her, she knows without a shadow of a doubt that no Edenian will be foolish enough to venture out to meet her before daybreak. By then, she's convinced, she'll be a lost cause.

Electra J. is convinced that she has been followed for hours by shadows that seem to adhere to the grooves of her wheels as surely as acid sludge sticks to the body of a car. When the engine stops, the entire air recycling system is interrupted. "Interior atmosphere at 26% breathable," says the on-board computer.

When the air in the cabin is staler than outside, you'll have to decide to get out. To die of hunger and thirst, or to die of asphyxiation, or to die at the hands of those who spy on her… "What ridiculous endings for the daughter of the most powerful man on the planet!"

The headlights go out. It's pitch black. Not a breath of air. Not a sound. Electra J. snatches the detachable flashlight from the dashboard and turns it on.

At least I'll have light until daybreak, she thinks, trying to reassure herself.

She should probably leave her sanctuary in search of less hostile lands, but her whole being tells her to stay where she is.

Here, at least I have water and food… It's true that this won't last forever, but

172

at daybreak the Edenians from Rotterdam will come to meet me. If I leave the car, without supplies, I don't have much chance of survival.

However, Electra J. is finding it increasingly difficult to breathe.

"Quantity of oxygen in the interior air: 17%." Nothing else indicates the quality of oxygen outside the car. Should it open or remain enclosed?"

Thinking, moving, everything seems harder than ever for Electra J. She's out of options, she's got to get out of here, find somewhere to breathe. She has to make up her mind… she has to get up… Electra J. falls unconscious onto her seat, the vehicle's doors wide open.

When Electra J. opens her eyes, she first imagines herself in a hospital room in the Dutch residence: everything around her is white, clean and silent. And then she slowly comes to her senses.

She couldn't be in a hospital, having left the Eden residence hours ago. She was stopped in the middle of nowhere and the perpetual motion of her car had stopped. No air, NO AIR!

Her eyes now wide open, she tries to stand up and realizes that her wrists are tied to the bed.

Electra J. then starts screaming from her jail, out of anger and fear.

The door opens, a rancid smell announces the arrival of a man approaching her, his eyes inquisitive and his face deformed by appalling scars. She is petrified with horror.

"No need to shout, Lady, we mean no harm; we're just being cautious. You're the first person we've come across since our escape from the Brussels Megapolis. So you must be from there. Where were you going and how did you get this vehicle?"

Electra J. is stunned by what she sees and hears and can't think of anything to say; this man's way of expressing himself has absolutely nothing to do with his looks. His broken face and rugged complexion collide in Electra J.'s foggy mind.

The man softened a little. "What's your name? I'm the sedentary in charge of the Weert rehabilitation center; my name is Winston."

Winston is on his guard, but he immediately realizes that violence and threats are not necessary against this stray doe. This is no sedentary, let alone homeless, doe. She's well built but seems to come straight from another planet. Her mannerisms, right down to the way she's afraid, make her unlike any other.

Electra J. thinks it's the kind of facility that used to house and train homeless people before they returned to society as sedentary people. So she's probably safe.

However, prudence dictates that she keeps her identity to herself. After all, she is the daughter of the man responsible for the greatest genocide in human history, and she is speaking to one of the few survivors. She knows nothing about these people; they were more a concept than anything else, and now that she's met one of them, Electra J. even wonders if her father wasn't right to want to rid the planet of this rabble. She smiles, as if to help her get rid of this bad thought. Winston is not indifferent, and that motivates her a little. So she chose to use her middle name.

"My name is Julia," she says.

This seems to surprise and please Winston.

All the better if it works in her favor.

She'll try to say as little as possible.

"I decided to flee the Eden residence."

"Eden Residence?" he asks, obviously unaware. "What's this?"

Electra J. is even more surprised than he is… He doesn't know what Eden residences are. The sedentary people were even more ignorant about what governed them than she could have imagined.

"This is housing on the outskirts of megacities, after the great purification…"

Winston interrupts. "The great purification, but what are you talking about?"

Electra J. breaks out in a cold sweat. She can feel the beads of perspiration running down her back. She'll have to consider everything she says.

"That's what the authorities have called the restructuring of populations around the world," she adds, a little hesitantly. "A sort of plan to save mankind," she says, embarrassed to have to "sell" Nucleus's diabolical plan to the very people who should have paid for it.

"Saving? What the hell are you talking about? I've been to Brussels and found nothing but mass graves," Winston murmurs petulantly.

What happened there happened somewhere else?

It's amazing; he has no idea, Electra J. observes again in silence.

"I don't know much more than you do, but it seems that what you witnessed in Brussels has happened in all the Cartel cities," she concludes.

"This is terrible," Winston mutters.

He sits up slowly, without really thinking about it, as if the weight of his thoughts were more than his legs could bear. He remembers, as he often does at night in his nightmares, the piles of decomposed humans, the unbearable stench wafting from them and contaminating the whole city.

"I'll never forget what I saw in Brussels. How many perished? How many others were hunted down and shot afterward? I don't understand what happened; it makes no sense," Winston continues to mutter, almost to himself and full of guilt. "Of course, the busers had an illicit activity, but nothing that could justify such a massacre."

"Big Brothers spoke of a coup d'état, a regime change, on a global scale. The world we know is no more," continues Electra J. Winston remained silent.

True, he hadn't watched his MMC for long before he'd had to flee town. He must have missed the report. The sadness and incomprehension in this busted face's eyes almost move Electra J. "I don't know anything more" she said lying to her teeth, "I was in hiding for over a year to escape the massacre, and as soon as I could, I took my chances and ran. Without you, I'd probably be dead," she adds.

Her story is purely none sense and couldn't convince anyone, but Winston isn't listening anyway and taking advantage of his silence, she graces him, this time quite consciously, with the most charming smile possible and then resumes.

"Now that we've gotten to know each other, perhaps you'd be kind enough to untie me and maybe even show me around the center. How many of you are there?"

Winston can't seem to come to his senses, and Electra J.'s questions bounce off him like acid raindrops. She speaks calmly, but can't quite get used to the sad, deformed face that shamelessly presents itself to her. She has never seen anything more repulsive than the ill-fitting flesh that prevents this man from speaking clearly for too long.

"About sixty," he answers Electra J.'s question with some delay. After a long moment of silence, he adds, more to himself than to her, "There were a lot more, but many have died or disappeared."

"Have you had any births?" asks Electra J. matter-of-factly.

"Yes, fortunately," replies Winston naively.

Without bothering to look at Electra J., who was wavering between disgust and relief, Winston releases her wrists from the restraints and invites her to follow him.

176

Sedentary people are not infertile, thinks Electra J.

"Christ, the Eden residences are seceding from our government one after the other. They have broken off all communication with us and disconnected from AGORAPP. We are no longer able to enforce the common policy. I believe that the disappearance of your father and the suspicions surrounding his death have definitively won over our last loyal followers."

"Can't you make an effort to bring me better news? There are just over a hundred million of us on this damn planet and we're still not able to get along?"

Pierre, now Christ's right-hand man, doesn't know what to say. It's not easy to advise someone who only wants to hear what suits him… Ever since his father's death, Christ has been power-mad: he wants to take over, he feels Eden needs a firm government to put things right, and he believes he's the only one who can do it.

At the moment, the residences have neither weapons nor means of transport, but without a common policy, it's only a matter of time before one of them finds the solution to obtain both. We have to be the first.

Christ turns to Pierre.

"Find me those who can help us."

Pierre exits the meeting room almost mechanically.

What allows everyone to survive in the residence, and no doubt anywhere else on Eden, is the automatic equipment. They allow GMO plants to grow and water to be recycled. The plan was to take advantage of the planet's riches and cutting-edge technologies, allowing nature to regain its strength and the new population to organize itself. Pierre had come to understand this all too well by working with Nucleus. Day after day, he had come to understand and embrace his vision of society.

Now that Christ wanted to go another way, nothing really made sense.

As far as the actual labor force is concerned, the one that makes it possible to design, build or improve, there's no one left that he knows of. All Eden's residents are top civil servants, lobbyists, bankers and traders, all specialized in the art of making money out of money, but now that money is no longer a solution, they're left with problems that none of them can solve.

Assemble an army and build a tank? Drive it? Ha!

Pierre smiles nervously. Christ is crazy. The Nucleus project was based entirely on a unilateral agreement and a direct, controlled democratic government. Without it, those who possessed the power and resources on what was once Earth would kill each other off to the last man out of fear or ambition.

Despite a strict fornication policy, the population continues to dwindle in Belgian residence, as in every other residences on the planet, Christ is convinced.

The couple is no longer the image of the inaccessible island that everyone wants to present as the showcase of Edenian society. On the contrary, adultery was initially imposed after years of infertility to combat immunological incompatibilities. Very quickly, couples were made and unmade according to the most unbridled fantasies or the deepest depressions, with the almost always disappointed hope of conceiving.

What was once a haven of luxury and peace for elite families is now a place of sexual perversions and political conspiracies, where nobody trusts anybody and everybody screws everybody, literally and figuratively.

"At least when they're having sex, they're not plotting against me", Christ thinks.

He hasn't had sex for a long time or been physically active at all since his father died, and he's put on a lot of weight as he is consumed by guilt and remorse. He watches his father's gaze over and over again, like a sordid video he can't stop watching, the expression in his eyes as life slips out of his body. The brief moments of respite soon give way to frustration and hatred.

"Why do things keep happening the way they did in my childhood? Nothing's turning out the way I'd hoped. Everything was so easy for my father and sister, and nothing seems to spare me!"

Christ rages with frustration and powerlessness. He has definitely lost control and he knows it.

"We've had thirteen new deaths this morning: two suicides, ten from cancer and one woman who died giving birth to our only newborn," says Pierre, who has been waiting motionless in Christ's room for ten minutes, unable to get his attention. "Bringing the residence's population to…"

"Leave me alone," he exclaims as he leaves.

Outside, the residence is unrecognizable. The ground is littered with garbage, and the smell of compost encourages people to stay at home and mate.

"My father, that incorrigible idealist, should have kept a few privileged sedentary people to serve us."

Christ rants against his father but knows full well that such a thing had been considered, then rejected. Keeping the members of a subaltern society is the best way to create a possible nucleus of resistance that would be fatal to the new order, whose every means of military, police or armed repression had been eliminated.

Christ had to set up surveillance patrols around the automatic vegetable garden and water treatment plant to guard against possible looting or sabotage.

"Nucleus was wrong about his fellow residents! Edenians are just as savage and unscrupulous as sedentary people were when Eden was still called Earth."

On his way to the communication rooms to try once again to contact former Nucleus delegates from the other Eden residences of the cartels, Christ crosses a curiously quiet street. The only sounds are the moans of couples abandoning or crossing paths in the almost utopian hope of creating new lives.

After days of reflection, Winston finally decided to address the members of the rehabilitation center's community. They all recognize him as their leader, a role he loathes. It's true that he often feels he's the only one trying to anticipate problems. This time, however, he had sworn to himself that he wouldn't suggest anything, but it's high time he did, and his companions' cognitive abilities seem to be clouded by decades of organized stupidity and malevolent tutelage.

"The royal jelly reserves won't last forever, so it's unreasonable to stay in Weert indefinitely, waiting for the supplies to run out or for us to be driven out by some unknown predator."

Electra J. is no stranger to this position. Since they met, she's spent a lot of time with Winston. He's probably her father's age; she hasn't dared ask him yet. A lifetime of suffering has made him mature faster than he should have. But Electra J. has come to see beneath his weathered features and the huge scar, to see the finesse of a naturally elegant man. He made her feel better, less tormented.

She understands the reasons why the community has elected Winston as their representative. He doesn't have Electra J.'s education or culture, but he has a strong spirit and an impressive life force. She and Winston end up spending more and more time talking about increasingly personal matters. Electra J. wonders if this man isn't the only person with whom she's been truly sincere and who knows the most about her innermost thoughts.

Winston's relationship with Electra J. is of a completely different nature. He thoroughly enjoys his time with her, but something about her makes him uncomfortable. He has no words to describe this feeling, because he's never had the opportunity to experience the discomfort caused by too great a social difference between individuals.

So far, the few interactions that make up his social experience have only taken place with other sedentary people or SUBs. He has only met people who share his past and will live a future quite similar to his own. Although Electra J. is extremely cautious and never mentions any of the elements that make up who she is, these elements shine through in every one of his opinions and proposals. Even if her father no longer exists for her, any more than the Electra J. she used to be, even if she has succeeded in completely disregarding this past life, of which she has a distant memory, like the vague, painful reminiscences of a nightmare, the experience that forges her being remains. This unprecedented experience surpasses anything Winston has ever accumulated since birth and provokes this feeling of inferiority he can't shake off.

"I know from previous journeys that there is a tunnel linking each of the centers to the megalopolis of Brussels. I don't know if the railcar still works, but I do know that the distance could be covered by the train in less than an hour; even if it had to be done on foot, I think it's possible."

The idea of returning to the hell of the Megalopolis is unbearable for him. But there is an alternative to the anthropophagous mush they've been eating for so long, and he can't bring himself to ignore it any longer. Besides, if the Eden residences Electra J. has told him about really do exist, he wants a chance to find out. She's described luxury, vegetable gardens, the worldwide problem of infertility and the great cleansing, even if she hasn't told him about her father.

"We're going to randomly select the twenty or so of us who will take part in the expedition. No one is obliged to come, but it's essential that chance makes the first selection." Since they moved into the center, all the leaders have been chosen by lot. Winston is wary of leaders and their good intentions. Chance rarely chooses the same people, which leaves little room for evildoers to organize themselves.

A few hours later, the group was selected: eight men and twelve women headed for the subway train. Winston would have preferred more men for this undertaking, which would undoubtedly require some physical strength, but fate had decided otherwise and Electra J.'s presence by his side was the only thing that really mattered to him.

As on the previous occasion, the train lights up as the group approaches, the doors open and a loud hiss is heard. Everyone settles in as best they can because, for all concerned, this is a first.

This time, travelers won't have to pay with their blood, Winston thinks.

The doors close and the journey begins.

After forty minutes of running smoothly and without violence, the train gradually slows to a complete stop in the middle of the tunnel. After a few moments of immobility, during which looks of astonishment and fear are exchanged, the carriage shuts down, leaving the group in total darkness. A few have electric lamps and turn them on, but most have organized makeshift torches. There's no smell of gas, but no one dares to light them just yet.

Winston is no more reassured than his companions, but the pressure of other people's stares, Electra J.'s presence and his damned instinct for self-preservation push him back into action. He opens the doors of the train without too much difficulty, invites one of the lamp holders to follow him with his eyes, and the two of them step into the darkness.

The floor is curiously soft and the air is thick with humidity. Large drops drip from the ceiling of the tunnel and a completely new smell invades their nostrils. Something has changed, and the two men can sense it, but can't quite define it. They just hope it will be to their advantage; the group has been through so much already.

Not a sound in the carriage. Everyone watches the light from the electric lamp gradually fade, and some are already thinking of walking back to the center. No one plans to do it alone, so waiting is the only alternative.

Fortunately, Winston and his partner soon return.

Less than a hundred meters away, the road is blocked by a forest of roots. No one has ever seen anything like it, and no one knows what it is.

"What's all this stuff dangling and seeping through the tunnel vault?" asks a subway rider.

Of course, no one, except perhaps Electra J., can or intends to answer this question.

"The train won't be able to get through, but there's enough space between these things that we can continue on foot. We could also return to the center; it's up to you."

Electra J., guessing what Winston is up to, exclaims, "Aren't we going to stop at the first hurdle? These things you're talking about are plant roots, so there's no immediate danger. What I can't quite figure out is where they come from and which plant they belong to.

Although some would have gladly turned back immediately, no one dares to speak up, and everyone is already preparing to continue the expedition on foot.

Winston is, of course, on the front line.

"What the hell am I doing here," he says to himself as he steps cautiously between the roots, *"*I'm too old to be doing this sort of thing... I guess not!" he concludes in a low voice, cursing his fate.

After a few dozen meters, the forest of roots closes in, and it becomes increasingly difficult to move forward. Winston and his companions can almost feel them growing fast around them.

"Perhaps it would be more prudent to turn back," dares one of the companions.

Everyone was secretly hoping for such a proposal, and the majority soon rallied around the new project. Even Winston is delighted, and protests only mildly.

The group turns back, but after a few meters, everyone realized the gravity of the situation.

The roots, which were still widely spaced when they first passed through, are now so dense that it is impossible for the group to get around them. The roots are growing so fast that a solution has to be found very quickly if the expedition is not to become permanently trapped in this vegetal tangle.

"We'd have been better off going through the surface," mutters one of them.

"Have you seen the size of the roots? How do you think it looks from above? In my opinion, it's a real jungle," replies Electra J. with an uncharacteristic aggressiveness that she immediately regrets.

How would he know? She thinks.

"Maybe," retorts the first, "but at least we wouldn't be buried alive up there!" It's a remark that sends a chill down their spines.

"There's only one thing to do," Winston curtly interrupts, his self-preservation instinct taking over.

"The tunnel ceiling must be badly damaged—the whole thing could collapse at any minute," exclaims another.

That's all it takes to create panic within the group.

Winston, without saying a word, gets down on his stomach and starts to crawl between the roots, which have not yet completely pierced the pavement and are easy to move. The issue is that there are a lot of them, and more and more.

Without any real transition, the band goes from collective hysteria to extreme concentration. No one finds the situation funny and everyone proceeds methodically through their grueling ordeal.

Within minutes, their elbows and knees were bleeding, and only the surplus sap, flowing generously from the roots and coating the uneven surface with its syrupy consistency, managed to give them a little relief.

The plant blood, gradually mixing with their own, soon affects them with gentle indolence. The group slows down.

"Sap tastes good. It's good to eat," says one of the creepers.

It's hard to imagine what it would be like to have eaten nothing but recycled dead bodies all your life, only to discover the taste of what could be likened to maple syrup. Time stands still or becomes elastic, as does this new nectar that everyone is now tasting and enjoying.

"*Worms, we've become worms!*" Thinks a terrified Electra J.

As best she could, she tried to squeeze through the ever-tightening roots. At first, she tried to stay as close to Winston as possible, but this soon proved impossible. How could she follow any plan in this shifting maze of roots and sap? It was no longer possible to crawl under the vegetation. Now Electra J. zigzags between the roots, carried along by them, with no notion of up or down, on the lookout for the slightest gap that might allow her to advance toward the light. Unlike the others, Electra J. has only ingested small quantities of sap. This sticky, gooey substance hardly inspires her. She remembers with great emotion what was offered to her in Eden, and this ersatz food is not even a pale copy. Yet already she feels numb. There's something wrong with her perception. She's convinced she's been drugged by this plant invader and it's getting harder and harder to fight the drowsiness, yet she keeps going.

Winston, on the other hand, hasn't made any progress for a while; his eyes unfocused, he can't see the roots encircling him, nor the sap level rising dangerously. His mind wanders and digresses far from these material considerations. He recalls boarding school and his upbringing in a cell, the first time he entered what was to be his sedentary "cage," his wild nights with the busers, his escape, his probable death… and always, as a leitmotif, his fascination for the beautiful Serena, whose image is brushed by his thoughts.

How beautiful she is. How he desires her right now. He'd spent so many years fucking women, and it's been so many years since he's had one. He imagines his siren in the outfit she wore the first time he saw her on a Big Brother show. He corrects in his mind what might have been their meeting when he was transfixed and totally at her mercy. She speaks to him through the screen.

"Come now," she summons him.

He doesn't resist, nor does he question the plausability of the situation. As he stands still for far too long, she crosses the screen and approaches him in slow steps, without taking her eyes off him, like a predator feasting on its prey and wanting the pleasure of waiting to last. He's speechless. His sedentary outfit sticks to his skin, dripping with desire. Suddenly he realizes that his ankles and wrists are restrained. He knows he's doomed, yet the prospect of contact with this woman he doesn't really know but has dreamed of for so long triggers an erection so intense it's painful. She now touches him at the epicenter of the pain. He is electrified and his whole body trembles with excitement. He wishes he could break free of her bonds, but the physical and psychological ascendancy she has over him at this moment forbids him any latitude. His gaze proudly supports that of his assailant, who buries her hands even deeper in the foundation of his manhood and tears away the remnants of the fabric armor still protecting him without the slightest difficulty. She holds him by the penis like a dog on a leash, coaxing him to lie obediently on a mattress of vegetation, displaying his organic sundial to the glory of her adoration. She indiscriminately massages his penis, his balls and impertinently slips a finger into his sap-soaked anus, straddling the face of her martyr.

He lets out a moan of pleasure and astonishment, then, still bound hand and foot, plays with his tongue, finally succeeding in parting the twin lips of his torturer's femininity to reveal the electric button of his secret pleasures. She shakes off her own burden of cotton and reveals, panting, her divine nipples enthroned atop the two maternal muses that adorn her body, studded with drops of desire. With a flick of her loins and without taking her eyes off Winston's sex, she offers her ass to be licked as she slides two of her fingers into her moist pussy. Serena flinches with pleasure and her legs give out on her.

With his path thus cleared, the opportunist takes advantage of the situation to intrude, headfirst, on the periphery of his beauty's foundation and with his nose in her nectar, he devours her sanctuary of inverted pleasures. Serena can take no more, and with a shuddering moan, she unleashes a fountain from which her tormented victim loses not a drop. But Winston is too quickly submerged, suffocating and struggling to breathe…

The pain brings him back to his senses for a moment. The sap has almost completely invaded the tunnel and it's nearly impossible to find air to breathe. His body still heavy and his brain foggy; he does what it takes to free himself from his shackles. A few meters away, the concrete ceiling has given way to the power of this new nature. The acidic, parched desert soil of the countryside revealed, in this way, eventually crumbles, collapses and disappears in the molasses, which doubles in volume and fully submerges Winston.

The plants on the surface immediately invade the tunnel, freeing a window of light, which he manages to reach and crawls to the surface. As for Electra J., the tidal wave of vegetation caused by the collapse of the tunnel catapulted her against some of the more resistant roots, and she lost consciousness a few hundred meters from the line's terminus station.

In the communications room, the screens are hopelessly black, and the loudspeakers repeat over and over the same message recorded long ago by Christ. Initially intended for Nucleus's former confidants scattered around the planet's other Eden residences, whom he hoped to rally to his cause, this message gradually turned into Christ's distress call to nothingness. The very illustration of his inability to captivate and unite the Edenians as his father had done.

He would almost have preferred this blackout to be the result of technical problems, but the components intended for Nucleus and his ilk have been designed to be indestructible, unlike those manufactured for the sedentary, with their programmed obsolescence. As a result, everything works perfectly inside the residence, and no one is skilled enough to be able to cut off outside communications.

Undoubtedly, Chris is alone on either side of the residence's protective dome.

Lost in the darkness of his thoughts, he mechanically twirls the office chair he's sitting in, as if to illustrate the infernal spiral Eden is in.

I'm going to die from owning too much, drowning in my possessions, suffocated by hard-earned power. An entire planet is at my disposal, and I am unable to enjoy it as I see fit.

At that moment, he shudders at the image of a virus taking over a body to the point of annihilation, then disappearing with its last breath.

We're parasites, he thinks.

A terse message appears on his watch, a break-in in progress in the vegetable garden; a large part of the production is compromised.

That's all it took to bring Christ back to less esoteric considerations: Those jerks are breaking the plate they're eating from and nobody cares?

He's beside himself, his eyes shining with anger and frustration. He rushes

191

out of the communications room, storming down the stairs to the outside of the building, under the starry vault of the dome. Without slowing down or stopping, he passes the closed doors of the residence's theater. It was then that he felt his first wave of pain shoot through his chest. He'd never been much of a sportsman, but since his father's death, with the added stress and frustration, he'd drunk a lot and put on a lot of weight. He pauses for a moment to catch his breath when another wave of pain, sharper this time, forces him to sit up.

Even his body fails him.

The garden's not far, he thinks, I should still be able to get there.

A few more meters, but now he's crawling along, holding his chest. He can see the edge of the vegetable garden. Of course, those who were supposed to be standing guard aren't there; it's women, lots of women, who are gathered in front of the entrance. He doesn't know them all, but he recognizes Serena, the famous singer who had managed to join the camp of the more fortunate after the support she had given to "Jouvence."

I've never liked her, he thinks.

After observing him for a few seconds, she approaches him slowly. He tries to question her about her unusual presence when she strikes him. He's superficially wounded, but enough to bleed. He stares at her, bewildered. She's just attacked him with a table fork! If he hadn't already been in such a bad way, he'd probably have laughed his heart out.

The great Christ, son of Nucleus, was struck down by a woman armed with a fork. It's only a moment later, and probably a little too late, that he realizes the presence of all the other women around him.

One after the other, with all their strength, they hit him with their kitchen weapons. He is instantly overwhelmed. Hit in the eye, the belly, the sex and the throat, several times in a thick silence without anyone uttering a word.

Christ collapses in a pool of blood.

When Winston comes to his senses, lying on a strangely cool, damp floor, he sees nothing but green.

Green and purple.

High above him, between the intertwined leaves and the bouquets of six-petaled flowers, he glimpses the white of the sky. He has undoubtedly emerged from the tunnel and is on the surface. Once consciously reassured of his immediate fate, his next thought is for Electra J.

I want to have a chance of finding this residence! Winston couldn't put into words the emotions that overwhelmed him when he thought of her. Or even worse, when he imagined her buried alive, hemmed in by that forest of roots that had so nearly gotten the better of him. He hadn't really realized it yet, but Electra J. represented for him the hope of a possible tomorrow.

Despite the combined forces of pain from his wounds and emotion, he is stunned by the vision before him: the last time he was in the rural desert around the Weert rehabilitation center, there was nothing but acid mud and desolation. The vegetation now invading the area must have done so in a matter of weeks.

His thoughts are again drawn to Electra J.'s face. Impossible to reach her. Impossible even to know if she's still alive. He has little interest in the fate of others, but Julia is a different matter. He has to know; he has to be sure. His future depends on it.

To continue in this vegetable hell is absolutely out of the question. It's impossible to find one's way; there are no landmarks.

How could a plant invade the land in such a short time? He continues to wonder.

He knows that he can't stay put indefinitely. As always in critical situations, immobility is ultimately fatal.

It's at this moment that Winston perceives a slight buzzing sound. He hadn't distinguished it at first. The wind in the young shoots produces a gentle rustling of foliage that is, for Winston, a veritable deafening cacophony. All he knows of the outside environment is dead nature and abysmal silence. He soon becomes convinced that it's a mechanical hum, and that only humans use machines; although the risk is great, his only chance of survival at this moment is to rejoin his fellows, hoping not to be greeted with stones.

It will take him hours to fight this new jungle. Every meter he gains is at the cost of insane efforts. He's like a tiny insect in the middle of a field of tall grass, but he's obviously not physiologically equipped for such a challenge. He tears his hands, knees and elbows on contact with the foliage, and with each cut Winston loses his vigor, feels nauseous and dizzy, only the will to find Electra J. keeps him going.

The properties of plants are very different from those of their roots. He feels that every time he comes into contact with them, he poisons himself further, but he also knows that if he gives up the fight, he'll die out there, in the middle of nowhere. He pushes aside the leaves, pulls himself up between the stems, stumbles and tears his face as he falls among this flora as supple as it is passively hostile. If he had a tool or a blade to help him, he might have a chance, but how could he unravel such a labyrinth with his bare hands?

Blinded by his own blood, limbs and face lacerated like a martyr of Christianity, Winston crawls more than he walks. Half-unaware, he bumps into something smooth and cool that seems to rise even higher than the vegetation.

For a moment, this soothing contact gives him back some of his strength, as his whole body begs for a little of this freshness. Then he loses consciousness, standing face down on the polymethyl methacrylate dome, wedged between nature in revolution and the Eden residence, an anachronistic symbol of a dying civilization.

Winston opens his eyes, and half a dozen female faces are bent over him to witness his awakening. In spite of himself, this vision reassures him, although he can't really explain it to himself.

"You've been poisoned by the foliage of this new species of Pontederia crassipes, the Water Hyacinth," explains Maria, one of his benefactors. "But obviously, it doesn't just grow on water anymore," she adds with a perfectly irrelevant smile.

"But... I..." Winston inspects the parts of his body he can see and scans his thoughts for any pain. He doesn't know how long he's been unconscious, but probably long enough to be effectively treated and healed.

"Do you know who caused this plant cataclysm?"

Another continues, "Not precisely. We simply know that, after the great pollution and desertification of the last rural areas in 2050, the cartels chose to plant a genetically modified species of Pontederia crassipes[viii]. This species drains the land of heavy metals and pesticides. The project produced mediocre results, and the plantations quickly dried out on all sites. The company responsible for modifying the plant's genes, on the other hand, had made billions. I'm in a good position to know, as my father was at the time the CEO of the African Green Clean division, which..."

"How are you feeling?" interrupts the first women.

I must be in one of those residences Julia was talking about, Winston thought.

He's not sure what to do next: answer the question meekly or find out a little more to be sure.

"None of the men in your community are interested in my recovery," he questions with what little humor he's managed to accumulate since the beginnings of his social life. He does so in the hope of getting some details about the community's configuration without being too inquisitive.

"There are only women here," replies Maria, who appears to be the group's spokeswoman.

That's when Winston realizes that he's tied up on a bed.

"What do you want from me?" he continues, in all seriousness this time.

"I think we'd be better off asking you the same question: where did you come from? It's impossible to get around this jungle on foot, and there's nothing around the residence, so how did you get here?"

Without responding to the question, and with a deliberate pause to stir their curiosity, Winston presses on "I was with a woman; did you see her? She knows about your community, she's hiding there, her name is Julia."

The women look at each other blankly.

"I have no desire or interest in being aggressive," he continues. "It's probably in your interest too; if you don't know her, she knows you. She also knows where I'm from, having lived there too. She'll be able to convince you better than I can that we have to go looking for her!" Winston's tone is higher than he would have liked and, after an exchange of glances, the women leave the room.

My interactions with mankind inevitably end up poorly, he thinks helplessly, and tugs angrily at his bonds, which tighten even more.

Julia was well ahead of him in the tunnel, he was certain. She had to get out before he was submerged; that would be too bad. He had to convince them to go looking for her.

Seized by a powerful rush of rage, Winston starts to scream.

Calmly, the group of women re-entered the room and moved silently in his direction. He briefly feels a prick on his thigh, and all is misty again.

"Shall we get rid of him? Not only is he repulsive, he's also violent," suggests one of the girls, who's probably fed up.

"We didn't pamper him for that long just to get rid of him as soon as he woken up, so he'll calm down eventually. He's got a really ugly mug, poor guy, but I think he's got the rest of the anatomy of a breeder, don't you? On this subject, we must leave no stone unturned, as so far, our experiments with the youngest of our men have ended in terrible failures. I'm also intrigued by this woman's story and would like to know who she is. Did she live here? As far as I know, the only one to have left the residence before our government was the sister of that coward Christ. But her name is Electra, not Julia.

"I'll go and tell Serena that the patient has finally woken up.

After several hours, the product introduced into Winston's bloodstream is still active and his ideas are more than confused. It takes a moment before he realizes that the person sitting at his bedside is Serena.

He must be dreaming, because she's holding his hand! His gaze slides from one hand to the other, from one arm to the other, and continues its course to his visitor's face. There's no doubt about it, the woman of all his young sedentary fantasies is just a few centimeters away from him and seems to take no notice of his condition. The years barely register on her. She's eternally young, eternally beautiful.

"I… I… Serena," he stammers like a child caught in the act.

"Do you know me? I'm very flattered," she replies, falsely modest and smiling. "Perhaps you've seen me on the screens?" she continues, going beyond the limits of bad faith.

Winston doesn't analyze anything, of course, and is already having a hard time properly assessing the situation and what's at stake.

"I never missed any of your appearances Madam, I…," he said, as childish as he was sincere.

"How nice of you to say that," replies Serena, well versed in the art of false modesty inherent in her profession.

"Maybe I even owe you my life," he adds, as his mind regains a little independence.

"And why is that?" she said, genuinely surprised.

"I believe that, without you, I would never have decided to take Jouvence, and without Jouvence, I would certainly be dead today." Winston alludes to the state of physical decay he was in at the time, but Serena immediately thinks of the holocaust that followed the destruction of the African continent and the billions who died.

She had never imagined that Jouvence could one day save anyone's life, but this sentence allows her to better assess her interlocutor:

He's a former sedentary, certainly a Buser who managed to escape from the Megalopolis before or during the Great Purification. He has resources; we must continue his interrogation. Perhaps he knows an alternative to this hopeless residence.

"Serena, you're so beautiful…" Winston articulates as impressed children can when a powerful thought crosses their mind.

"Stop flattering me now, would you?" she resumes with the experience that comes with being a revered artist. "Tell me about this person you mentioned to my friends."

Winston immediately comes to his senses. "Of course, what an idiot! I was with someone, and we were in one of the subway tunnels that links the rehabilitation centers to the Metropole. We were invaded by roots from nowhere. I managed to reach the surface before the entire basement was invaded."

"Who was with you?" Serena asks curtly.

"A woman who has lived in a residence like yours."

"Who else?" interrupts Serena as curtly as ever.

"Others were sedentary people, a few homeless. We tried to reach Brussels in the hope of finding other survivors or some semblance of government organization.

"You've found us, my good man, and I assure you our little community wasn't worth your trouble," she concludes, no longer masking her disdain for Winston, exacerbated by disappointment.

So there's nothing better than this fucking shithole! Serena thinks to herself, exasperated with this entire situation.

He suddenly remembers conversations with Julia and the enthusiasm she had shown when discovering the community's newborns and takes a chance.

"We were lucky enough to have a few births," he ventures shyly.

"Births?" continues Serena, once again interested.

"Yes, why?" replies Winston, testing the limits of his lying skills.

"Where are these people?"

"We have to get back to the Brussels Megalopolis, which is where we arrived. It's the only way to get back to Weert." Winston hoped that Serena wouldn't remember that, only moments before, he had described the subway tunnel as inaccessible. In any case, Serena's brain has been in far too much turmoil since the start of their conversation to have dwelt on the detail of a story that had seemed so trivial and unimportant.

"OK, let's find out; if these women manage to go to term, there may be some hope."

Electra J. wanders through the rubble of the Ministry of Welfare. It's the first time she's seen vegetation from the surface, and what she sees is petrifying. All the walls, whether collapsed or still standing, are covered in this invasive flora, and the tiles on the floor are swollen with roots.

How many hours or days have passed since she lost consciousness, she has no idea. The sharp pain that ripped through her arm as she tried to stand up makes it clear that she didn't escape the tunnel unscathed. A wave of panic makes her waver. She doesn't think she's adventurous, nor does she imagine herself brave. She owed her boldness to Winston and his group. Now she's alone. Alone and wounded.

"I'm dying of hunger and thirst; I don't give myself two days before I give in to despair," she thinks aloud. "I'll try to get upstairs. If Winston's alive, maybe I can see him…"

She chooses the staircase that's easiest to reach and least invaded. She soon discovers the old refectory in the building, which contains what, for her, is nothing less than gold: water and cans of food.

After restoring herself, it takes all her tenacity to reach the rooftops of the Ministry, but when she does, the vision is phantasmagorical.

The vegetation grows in a star shape from different points in the city.

"Hills of green in the middle of what must be the remains of streets; it doesn't make sense," she mutters.

Some arms join the arms of another vegetation star in a vast, uniform green carpet that covers everything in its path.

Every day, she scans the horizon to her heart's content, on the lookout for the slightest movement, the slightest clue that might give her hope.

In this gentle, timeless torpor, and if the situation hadn't been so desperate, she would undoubtedly have taken some pleasure in admiring the changing landscape every day. Every morning, less and less desert and almost no concrete, mud or garbage. All that remains is a thick, ever-expanding blanket of chlorophyll, topped by a multitude of tiny purple dots. Nature has regained the upper hand, and the spectacle it offers is as beautiful and terrifying as an atomic explosion.

Slowly her mind digresses and fogs over, as if to protect itself, and more and more frequently she dozes off and even falls asleep on the roof, against one low wall or another, surrounded by her few precious cans and bottles of water that never leave her side.

When she wakes up, the sun had set, and a different sight is awaiting her.

The air is different, fresher, crisper, thinks Electra J., struggling for adjectives to describe how she feels. Then, with a sigh of relief, she gulps down all the air her lungs can hold but suspends for yet another moment, the moment when she must release the vital gas.

At this very moment, she's possessed by the very essence of life. She can't remember feeling this good in her entire life.

The wind caresses the foliage illuminated by a full, silvery moon. When night falls, all sounds are magnified, and she'd never heard the sound of the wind in the foliage, for the simple reason that there was no wind under the dome. Moonlight, meanwhile, makes the corollas of Pontederia crassipes almost phosphorescent. Electra J. doesn't yet know that this plant has become the planet's new dominant species.

She's no longer hungry; her arm gives her some respite and suspends the pain from her shoulder; she feels strong, and all her senses are alert.

It's into this fleeting euphoria that the mechanical noises of an approaching machine intrude, like a stain on a masterpiece. It's still a long way off, but the din, however distant, makes Electra J.'s happiness vanish, and her fears take over again.

Avoiding what she has diagnosed as a dislocated shoulder, she stands up as quickly as she can and tries to unravel the secret of the night, aided by a twinkling, complicit moon.

The mystery is easy to solve. Betrayed by headlights desperately trying to illuminate a road that no longer exists, an imposing vehicle from anachronistic construction sites forges a path through the dilettante and sovereign vegetation that willingly sacrifices some of its many branches.

Electra J. is certainly not going to leave her strategic high ground. If it's an enemy, this privileged position is priceless. If it's Winston or one of his companions in misfortune, the Ministry is located at the gateway to the city. There's no other way to enter the ruined city than to pass in front of it, and indeed, in front of her.

The crew moves with disarming ease and reaches the outskirts of the city in just a few minutes.

Winston knows where the mouth of the subway tunnel is, he knows Julia and he knows that she would never venture out of this providential refuge.

He's sure to find her.

Curiously, the closer the vehicle gets to the Brussels Megalopolis, the denser and more resistant the vegetation becomes, to the point where the perpetual motion engine is showing worrying signs of overheating. The plant wraps itself around the axles, and the wheels struggle to turn on their axles to make headway on a road that is now hopelessly buried under the Pontederia crassipes.

Suddenly, without the slightest hesitation, the front of the truck plunges into a gaping trap, open to the bowels of the town and concealed by the foliage. Everyone is taken by surprise. The passengers are thrown forward in shock, with neither the means nor the time to protect themselves. Nevertheless, the hole is narrower than the vehicle, and the bodywork squeaks against the asphalt walls to the limit of its elasticity, finally coming to rest like an unlikely edge in this mineral esophagus.

Winston climbed out through the rear window, which had been shattered in the accident. The two women, seated in the front, cling to their seats with the energy of despair, their feet through the shattered windshield and dangling over the dark, patient abyss. Serena manages to haul herself up to Winston, who is standing on the passenger compartment, and finally joins him, rather disconcertingly. Maria, on the other hand, is a very Edenian mother who has only taken up fitness and diets to meet the needs inherent in her social rank. She lacks his muscle tone and sways gently to the cadence of the creaking sheet metal, already feeling the strength in her hands failing her. Serena, still lying on the rear window, grabs her under the armpit, taking some of the weight off her shoulders. Winston takes off his shirt and hands her one of the ends of the garment, which is easier to grip than the thick seat. Maria managed to grab hold of it, and the combined efforts saved her. The three survivors regain their composure before jumping out of the vehicle onto the Pontederia crassipes layer, in which they immediately disappear.

Maria is petrified with fear. She's not cut out for this kind of misadventure, and even less for risking her life.

For her part, Serena has struggled all her life in the society of the haves, as she must now do in this new jungle. Little has changed for her, and she's adapting very quickly to her new environment.

"The thickness of the vegetation is absolutely terrifying," she says.

"Yes, and it looks even denser in that direction, but unfortunately, that's the way to go," adds Winston.

Maria screams hysterically, "I refuse to take another step!"

Maria is dripping with sweat, her whole body shaking like a leaf. She looks like she's just stepped out of a swimming pool. Never in her life had she experienced such a moment of fear. In fact, come to think of it, she'd never in her life felt anything outside the norm dictated by the size of her wallet.

"But you'll have to," Serena continues, "unless you want to stay here and watch the plant grow, dying of hunger and thirst…"

Maria is devastated and must face the facts: her ordeal has only just begun.

"I know this area," says Winston, "I've walked this road before it was overgrown. We're just a stone's throw from the Ministry, but we're going to need a new means of transport if we're to reach the Weert rehabilitation center or even get back to the residence. I know that one of these perpendicular streets hides an old sperm bank bus; it used to stand next to one of the city's countless mass graves."

Maria looks at Serena, not quite sure whether to rejoice at the prospect of salvation or to be appalled.

The group moves cautiously in the direction indicated by Winston, as they all know the effects of the scratches caused by Pontederia crassipes. For this very reason, they eventually give up their plan, as the plant erects a perfectly impassable wall of vegetation.

High above them, but at a distance that could not be reached on foot in these conditions, Maria and Serena stare in amazement at what they guess to be the mass grave earlier mentioned by Winston. Over it stands powerful vegetation, thick and bursting with life.

"I believe that the development of this filth is stimulated by the amalgam of sedentary people's blood, calcium, the abundance of pollution and mold concentrated in the Megalopolis. It's the only plausible explanation," says Maria, for whom water hyacinth seems to hold no secrets.

"It's disgusting," comments Serena, thinking of what could happen to her very soon. Humanity has become fertilizer to stimulate this green monster. "So much for the bus, we'll have to find another solution," she adds, turning back to Winston. "You know the area, take us to the Ministry instead.

Although movement becomes easier as the group moves further away from the mass grave, the plant is still incredibly abundant, making the undertaking arduous and perilous. No one speaks, all concentrating on their task, but Winston can't keep himself from looking at Serena out of the corner of his eye.

I'm walking next to Serena. The Serena, My Serena!

She was the closest he'd ever come to his feminine ideal. A kind of unattainable fantasy, she combined—or so he thought at the time—beauty, intelligence, talent and power. Now he walks beside her. Better still, she follows him; he guides her. What's more, her physical condition is quite remarkable. There's something unspeakable, though, something that's bothered Winston ever since their first meeting in his convalescent room; a certain coldness and a real hardness in her eyes that he'd never perceived before when she appeared on his Big Brother. Winston is certainly intimidated, but almost as repulsed as attracted. And then the memory of his burning passion as a young man is not quite compatible with his current preoccupations, all centered around saving Julia.

"Look up there, isn't that the Ministry?" challenged Serena, pointing her finger in the direction of a building more imposing than the others, of which they could only make out the roofs.

"Yes, it is," confirms Winston.

Serena, suddenly motivated by this vision, picks up the pace a little and passes Winston.

How beautiful, he thinks, admiring the shape of his former idol. *What an airhead. You've got a face to scare, you're in the most dangerous green shit there is and the only thing you can find to do is to watch that ass go by...*

Maria, who is usually unbearably talkative, hasn't said a word since the truck accident. If Winston is surprised by this, it's more to find a way of changing the train of thought than out of any real interest in Maria.

Well, she's speeding up too… she can't be too keen on being dumped by Serena and finding herself alone in my company.

Winston, consciously or not, slows down slightly.

"Ladies," he says emphatically, "I'm going to try and find some food, I think I've got an idea."

"I'm going to look for a means of transport in the basement of the building. We'll meet at the main entrance," Serena replies without turning around.

"I'm with you," Maria almost cuts in.

Winston stands still, contemplating the forecourt of the Ministry. He hesitates to enter. He doesn't care about the food; he needs to find Julia alive. She's his ultimate asset. Without her, what he guesses to be an Eden residence will offer him only banishment or death. He thinks back wistfully to Catherine, to their conversation. He now realizes that what he had discovered with Catherine was only the beginnings of what a human relationship could really be. Even after leaving the Brussels Megapolis and gradually losing the mutual suspicions that infected any relationship between fugitives, they were quite incapable of doing what Julia was doing in talking with him. How could it be otherwise? He'd never had the slightest social relationship.

Winston's thoughts digress. Could she have had a social life? It seems inconceivable…

Sure, she'd had to hide for a year, she'd told him, in one of the privileged residences, but hiding didn't encourage social relationships. He didn't really pursue the matter, however, and she seemed intent on evading the subject as if to forget a bad memory. Winston had thought it wise to respect this choice, but in the end, while she knew him well, he knew rather little about her past.

He suddenly breaks out in an inexplicable cold sweat.

It doesn't take Serena and Maria long to find what they're looking for. One of the building's underground levels is entirely dedicated to service vehicles, and many of them are still in perfect working order, once the thick film of dust and ash has been removed.

"Well, we've got to get back to the monster now. Mark my word, he's too ugly to waste my time trying to find him. I'm already regretting enough that I willingly got myself into a mess like this to check out the incongruous story of this madman…".Serena hadn't deliberately gotten herself into this mess on presumptions. She knew full well that there was no future at the residence and that the only hope lay outside and would come from new encounters and new opportunities. She follows Winston's trail as she would any trail that might lead her to a possible way out of the sterile confines of the residence. If the trail leads nowhere, she'll find a way to get rid of Winston, his protege, if he finds her, and anyone elsc who gets in the way.

Maria doesn't agree with Serena at all.

She must have been in showbiz circles all her life; she became way too picky, she thinks of Serena.

Winston may be disfigured, but he exudes such masculinity that she shivers every time their eyes meet. Maria married a paunchy, flabby banker, thirty years her senior, who, in the end, had inspired nothing but disgust in her all these years without her allowing herself to think about it too concretely. She had high hopes of trying her luck with Winston and perhaps conceiving…it wasn't too late for her yet.

"I'll go back up to the main entrance and if he's not there, I'll look for him. There's not a sound; there's no way he won't hear me calling him. " Says Maria.

"In the meantime, I'll take the truck out of the garage. I'll wait for you outside. Don't be long!" responds the singer.

Winston wanted to convince himself that he knew where to find Julia, but now that he's at the Ministry, he doesn't know where to go. In endless, crumbling, plant-infested corridors, the reverberation of his footsteps breaks the oppressive silence at regular intervals. He ventures a timid "Julia," which is lost in the immensity of the deserted halls, which seem to go on forever.

He knows he has to do things differently. Try to think like her. What would he do in her place? Certainly not stay in this blood-curdling place. Since leaving the place is out of the question, the only possible and strategic place would be the roof.

Yes, that's certainly where she is, Winston reassures himself as he presses on toward what he thinks are the stairwells.

When he reaches the top of the building, he discovers a space as vast as the lower floors but instead of adjoining rooms, there are air-conditioning chimneys as far as the eye can see.

It's going to take me hours to search this place. I'm not even sure Julia's here, and the other two are just waiting to dump me here!

Lost in his gloomy thoughts, he walks slowly toward the balustrade that crowns the roof and protects the unwary from a fatal fall. Wherever he looks, the spectacle is the same: countless Pontederia crassipes Stars decorate the avenues of the Megapolis with their crisscrossing branches of chlorophyll. Each of these Stars has a human mass grave as its starting point, there's no doubt about it, the plant must have been over-stimulated by the considerable supply of fertilizer provided by the thousands of abandoned, half-burned bodies, and it's these putrid mountains that must have awakened the dormant Pontederia crassipes seeds and brought the plant back to life.

He recognizes Maria's distinctive, unpleasant, high-pitched voice. Moved by a sense of caution honed by years of precariousness and suffering, he silently advances toward where the sound is coming from. There's another voice, she's talking to someone, but whoever it is doesn't speak enough to be recognized, however he knows it's certainly not Serena. Maria never speaks to her in that tone. Winston remains under cover. "You can't imagine what's happened since you left," Maria said with that smile she knows how to use so inappropriately. "After your father was found dead in his room…"

In Electra J.'s horrified eyes, Maria suddenly realizes that in this foreword, she has just learned of her father's death, for which she was obviously totally unprepared.

"You didn't know, of course, it happened the day after you disappeared. The whole house was convinced that the two events were linked, and no one believed your brother's suicide theory. It could never be proven, but everyone remained convinced that Christ was the instigator of these events. Now that we've found you, I'm not as convinced… Perhaps we acted too quickly… There's no turning back now!"

Maria, openly embarrassed by her clumsiness, was becoming increasingly difficult for Electra J. to understand. What was she talking about? Acting too quickly? Going backward?

"How did he die?" Electra stammered, her eyes filling with tears.

Winston lights up, recognizing the voice at the first word, but remains cautiously under cover, wanting to hear the rest.

"The story we've been told is that he killed himself," Maria replies.

"Impossible," she asserted. "Times were hard, but he was in his element and the sole master aboard a ship he'd spent a lifetime building. He would never have taken his own life, especially not in the middle of a battle. It's murder," she concludes.

"Pretty much what everyone thought. Especially since, with your disappearance, all suspicions turned to Christ, who suddenly found himself with full powers, given the extreme precariousness of the political balance."

Electra J.'s senses are suddenly heightened. She is furious; she wants to know everything, to understand everything. The pain she feels when she realizes that she'll never again see the man she's fought so hard against, and who has shamed her so often, fills her with an unparalleled rage.

Winston recognizes the voice, but the tone and inflections are completely foreign to him.

"Since you left, there have been no births and it's the same in every Eden residence we've been able to get in touch with."

Electra J. listens, her eyes fixed, emotionless.

"Then, one by one, we ended up losing all communication with our partners. It's hard to know why." Maria answers the question no one was going to ask.

"Many disassociated themselves from the Nucleus project on learning of his death and his son's assumption of power. For others, perhaps technical or climatic problems. We know that one of the residences, just before our last exchanges, was invaded by vegetation."

"The vegetation," continues Electra J., "What happens here, happens elsewhere?"

"My dear, everywhere we've asked, the answer has been the same. This plant has literally invaded our world, and if we're not careful, Eden will turn into a gigantic jungle in which we'll have no place."

This time it's Winston who loops surprised.

What's Eden? What does she mean…

"And then the men started fighting again. Christ immediately abolished the semblance of democracy when he realized that the other Eden residences were disconnecting from AGORAPP one after the other, but he never had the ascendancy and charisma of your father. Soon everyone was claiming a political perennity that, in fact, belonged to no one! Even some women were in the game, and we locked them up with them…"

Neither Winston nor Electra J. could have imagined what Maria was about to say as she caught her breath and intentionally slowed the flow of her narration.

"When there is no longer any hope of new generations being born, when all hope of renewal is in vain, the few remaining children become the most precious beings, the ultimate salvation. We weren't going to let them be perverted without doing anything about it, as we'd always done up until now. This time it was too much," she said, stamping her foot like a capricious child. "Without really consulting each other, and talking about it like a funny story, we came up with a plan, and one thing led to another, and we put it into action."

"What are you talking about?" asks Electra J., hanging on her every word, but at a loss.

"The women first found a reason to bring all the residents together in the big theater." Maria takes a long break. "Then we closed the doors so that no one could get out."

She takes a breath. "We released gas through the ventilation system, and everyone lost consciousness."

It can't be! Now it's Winston's turn to wish Maria wouldn't go on but she did, very slowly and articulated.

"Then we entered the theater and eliminated all those whose thirst for power risked plunging our society once again into chaos and destruction."

Electra J. is speechless.

"The other men are still locked up in the theater, working on our reproduction experiments. They feed on the canned food we have conceded them. The children and young teenagers are still with us."

They're all sick, thinks Winston, clasping his head in his hands. She's talking about the perversion of children by the example of their fathers, and their first actions are murder and kidnapping.

"Maria, you talk too much!" exclaims Serena out of nowhere.

"You scared me," Maria exclaims. Then she continues, "Look whom I find on this roof: Electra J, the daughter of Nucleus. You probably remember her. She had disp—"

"Of course I remember her…" Serena interrupts softly as she reaches Maria, holding an imposing piece of glass wrapped in a rag. She swiftly cocked her arm and struck Maria in the throat with disconcerting speed and precision, leaving neither Winston nor Electra J. any time to react.

"And I certainly don't want her back at the residence, or even for anyone to know she's still alive. I've had it with the Orsons," she continues, now moving toward Electra J. frozen and in shock in more ways than one.

Without waiting, Winston throws himself at Serena to try and intervene, but she reacts swiftly and with one blow, cuts the hands he has wrapped around her neck. The pain forces him to let go, and now it's him she wants to attack.

"No witnesses, Quasimodo, that goes for you too!"

Winston is drunk with anger. He hates her for the insults that hurt him. He hates her for the sterile illusory love he bore her all these years. He hates her for the harm she wants to do to the one person in whom he placed all his hopes. He hates her for the betrayal he just discovered.

Just then Electra J. grabs one of the plastic water bottles she was keeping next to her and throws it in Serena's direction. Hit in the head, but not seriously, the ex-singer turns around and Winston, still on the ground, takes the opportunity to pull her violently toward him, throwing her off balance. She stumbled and hesitated for the moment Winston needed to grab a piece of wall and hit her relentlessly until every bone in her face was shattered. He would probably have continued if Electra J. hadn't started screaming.

On the way back, Winston didn't say a word while Electra J. told him everything.

For Winston, Earth or Eden, it didn't matter which planet so many people had suffered on. But if Electra J.'s father had been able to make such a decision, it was because his political power was immense.

How could I have been so wrong about Electra J.? He asks himself silently.

The car rolled right up to the gates of the residence, all around them and even on the dome, blocking out the sunlight, Pontederia crassipes has invaded the horizon. The residents' greatest fear is that it will creep under the dome walls. According to the most pessimistic hypotheses, this is how some of the other residences have been invaded: the dome cracks, then finally gives way and collapses on the inhabitants. The survivors can't resist for long in such a hostile environment.

No one but Maria knew the true motives behind the expedition. On their return, little justification is needed to explain the change of vehicle and to attest to Maria and Serena's death in the accident along with the others. Precariousness and danger make human lives less precious and their loss less unbearable.

Electra J. has her father's charisma, and as soon as the Edenians' surprise is over, the women listen to her and take into consideration what she shares with them.

The first thing she wants to do is visit the theater and hear what the people there have to say. Some of the women attempt to resist, but their efforts are half-hearted, drained of conviction before they even begin. They act like children who deny their exactions, hoping to make them disappear. But it's not easy to make thousands of people disappear, crammed into a building designed to hold half as many.

When Electra J. appears on stage, she is greeted by an almost funereal silence,

214

followed a few moments later by totally unintelligible howls of rage she could not manage. It's the very essence of any crowd to be incomprehensible, irrational and roaring. Nucleus abhorred them and intended to get rid of this shapeless, decerebrate mass by wiping out 99% of the world's population. Unfortunately, crowds, like poverty, are relative concepts that no one can get rid of. Not even the most powerful.

She can, however, recognize a few faces, ravaged by frustration, fatigue, hatred and the desire for revenge. She tries to intervene, but even her amplified voice can't pierce through the din of howling males blinded by vengeance. She gives up.

We need to change tactics.

First, to understand the situation, she must talk to the women who now run the residence. she must find out to what extent all communication with the outside world is compromised. she must see how the prisoners are being treated. Finally, she must find a way out of this inconceivable crisis.

Electra J. returns to the family estate to find the house's quite empty. Winston hasn't been allowed to follow her, but she knows he wouldn't have wanted to anyway.

She's on her own.

The day after his arrival, Winston didn't have a moment to rest. After his first night's house arrest in the type of luxury he could never have imagined, he was immediately put in the presence of the youngest and most receptive of the women in order to test his compatibility with the greatest number of candidates. His background and experience as a buser is invaluable in this respect, and the first few hours will remain in his memory and that of his partners as moments of near-nirvana delight. Unfortunately, his age and the absence of Jouvence eventually dried up the source of his enthusiasm.

He realizes, however, that, in humanity's current predicament, the only salvation is in their potential ability to conceive. He requests an audience with Electra J., which he obtains almost immediately.

When he enters what used to be Nucleus's home, Winston is seized by a shiver of dread. He can't comprehend anyone needing, or even wanting, to live in so much space, surrounded by so much furniture, invaded by so many objects. He scrutinizes the frames on the walls and the decorations on the parquet floor, without being able to name the paintings, the furnishings, the carpets or even the parquet floor. Everything is beautiful, even magnificent, impressive and intimidating, but why this excess? A body can only sit on one chair at a time, sleep on one bed at a time and wash in one shower.

Winston contemplates Electra's house with the incomprehension of a child admiring the immensity of a starry sky. While his mind quietly catalogs the space around him, Winston's attention is drawn to an object he immediately recognizes: a laser stylus, like the one Catherine had literally taught him to write with. The difference, of course, is that this isn't just one stylus. There are twenty of them. Winston approaches the collection, highlighted by indirect lighting and protected by a glass case. He carefully opens the glass cabinet door and takes hold of one of the pieces in the collection, engraved with the words, "To my son Christ, your loving mother."

In a flash, Winston remembers the man and child they had met when fleeing the Brussels Megalopolis. A mother and son. Electra J. and her father. Winston feels dispossessed. He hasn't known that love. He had no right to it. Without thinking, he grabs as many styli as his pocket will allow when suddenly:

"Winston, I'm glad you wanted to see me… I don't know how to apologize enough for not having been completely upfront with you since we first met, I…"

"Completely upfront?" Winston immediately exclaims, realizing at this moment the extent of his resentment toward Electra J., "but that's not the purpose of my visit," he continues. "For several nights now, your fellow citizens have been putting me to work. I have to admit that at first, the prospect of fooling around with this team of maternity candidates didn't displease me," he adds, in the almost unconscious hope of making her a little uncomfortable. "But this situation, however idyllic on the surface, can't last. The future and future generations cannot rely solely on my hypothetical compatibility with one of your kind. For years, busers and I have been filling burets and burets with sperm on buses. Have you tried artificial insemination?"

"Of course we have, Winston, come on!"

"So you're going to have to find a way to reconcile your males and females, because as far as I'm concerned, it's over."

Winston takes advantage of the long silence that follows his statement and waits a little longer than necessary before getting to the heart of the matter. The tension Electra J. is feeling at this moment is palpable and he doesn't want to relieve it too quickly.

"Have you thought about Jouvence?"

"What's your point?"

"My point is that there's no better way to get everyone back on the same page than with a good 'juvenation'."

"Jouvence has wreaked havoc among the sedentary population. I'd be too afraid of the consequences."

"Electra J., I had a front-row seat for the Jouvence for years and I know the effects. But it's the only alternative left. Otherwise, you'll have to think about

217

getting rid of those few thousand males they've stockpiled at the theater. The sleeping gas you're throwing into the aeration circuits isn't going to improve the sanitary conditions of these poor devils, or keep them down for much longer. At some point, they're going to break everything and make you pay for what you've done to them, unless you get rid of them before they get organized."

He pauses again to take in her defeated expression.

"But whatever the outcome, the surviving sex will have to wait helplessly for the race to die out."

He's right, these women have put themselves in a totally impossible situation, Electra J. thinks. There's really only the unlikely hope of reconciliation to save the day, and the best way to initiate dialogue between the protagonists is to force their desire.

"All right, Winston, we've got stock. You've no doubt learned since your arrival that my late father was head of the pharmaceutical company that marketed Jouvence. You should know that I've always op—"

"Guess what? I didn't know. In fact, the more time goes by, the more I realize that I didn't know anything about anything. Who did I work for when I was sedentary? What was my job for? How were our salaries financed, how were the laws that controlled our lives passed and enforced, and who financed the governments that enacted these laws? I wasn't even aware that residences like this existed. I thought everyone was affected by air pollution. Now I'm almost ashamed of my gullibility. For instance, do you know the true composition of the royal jelly that was your regular fare at the rehabilitation center?" Disgusted, Winston left the room.

Aerosolized Jouvence: Someone had to come up with it! Unwittingly, men inhale aphrodisiac vapors over several days and nights through air-conditioning ducts, which slowly transform them.

Since the start of his imprisonment and after the murder of Christ, Pierre has been nothing but fury and vengeance, and, like many others, has vowed to destroy his captors. Yet when Electra J. appears on the cinema screen above the stage, and the sound of her clear voice pierces the theater's speakers, he feels nothing but surprise, happiness, desire and passion. She's alive! Everyone thought she was dead, or at least permanently removed from the government of Eden.

The lights dim, and she begins to speak[ix].

"I'm sorry, but I don't want this situation; it's not my business. I don't want to punish or execute anyone. I'd like to help everyone as much as I can; there are so few of us already. We'd all like to help each other if we could; that's the way human beings are. We want to give happiness to our loved ones, not unhappiness.

"Envy has poisoned our minds, barricaded the world with hatred, and plunged us into misery and bloodshed. We've developed the mechanisms of power to the extreme, locking ourselves in. The machines that bring us abundance have left us dissatisfied. Endless calculation and intelligence have made us inhuman; we think too much and feel too little. We are too mechanized and lack humanity. We are too cultured and lack tenderness and kindness. Without these human qualities, life is nothing but violence and all is lost, but don't despair Edenians! Now that we're the people, let's not turn back into brutes, into a minority that despises, makes slaves and decides what to do and think, that rules and uses others as a negligible entity.

Let's not sacrifice our lives once again to this inhumanity; let's not become machine men again, with a machine for a head and a machine in our hearts. We are not machines! We are men and women, and we carry within us all the love in the world. We have no hatred, except for that which is inhuman, that which is not made of love.

"We, the people, have the power: the power to create these machines as much as the power to create happiness. We, the people, have the duty: the duty to give meaning back to our lives, the duty to do everything in our power to restore to our parched bodies and soils the ability to create life. We must no longer hate each other, we must no longer tear each other apart; we have so little time left; we must unite, we must desire each other, we must love each other to the last breath if we do not want to be the last representatives of the species.

"So, in the very name of love, let's use this power. We must fight together, not against each other, to bring about the new world dreamed of by so many and perverted by Nucleus. We can't erase the horror of what he did, but too many have suffered, too many have perished for this dream to escape us once again.

"So, we have to fight together, not against each other, to bring this world back to life, to put an end to greed, hatred and intolerance. We must fight together, not against each other, to build a world of reason and happiness, a world where science and progress go hand in hand with duty and responsibility. My friends, in the name of our survival, because it's our only chance of salvation, let us make love!"

The audience is in shock. Not a sound dares pollute the moment, and everyone hangs on the lips of Electra J., who remains motionless and silent, her gaze fixed on the camera. The shadow light drawn by the subdued lighting gradually brings the Edenians back to the absurd shores of the real world, where women have imprisoned and executed men, and where men dream only of revenge; a barren world with no future.

Like springs compressed since time immemorial and finally released, hearts unravel, and tensions subside. Hate is only the consequence of a state of mind and choice. At this moment, the crowd, no doubt inspired as much by Electra J.'s speech as by the vapors of Jouvence is ready to forgive and succumb to desire.

As if liberated by these new vibrations, the theater doors automatically release their locks. But no one takes any notice, for at the same moment Electra

J. appears like the Venus Anadyomene. She is carried by four equally naked young men whose glorious erections leave no doubt as to what is likely to happen next. They lay down their precious treasure for all to see and begin a long chorus of wandering caresses that tenderly transport Electra J. to bliss. The vibrations in the room become electric and the excitement is as palpable as the body of this new Aphrodite. When the long procession of Edenian women of childbearing age, beautiful and willing appears, almost levitating as they so carefully walk, the time stands still.

Overwhelmed by caresses and fiery kisses, Electra J. rambles,

"Nucleus, can you hear me? Wherever you are, look at me. Look at me, Nucleus! The mist is lifting. Light is breaking through. We're emerging from the chaos into which you plunged us to find the way. We're entering a new world, a better world, where everyone will dominate their greed, hatred and brutality with the forces of carnal desire. Look at me, Nucleus. Our soul has been given wings, and, at last, it's beginning to fly. It flies toward the rainbow, toward hope. Look at me, Nucleus! Look at me!"

Winston's idea was good. That Electra J. should get some glory instead of him is in the scheme of things, and he doesn't mind. He's tired of the pretenses, the power plays, lies and apartheid. He almost misses the days of his state instigated isolation as a sedentary and his innocent stupidity, programmed from birth. Unfortunately, now that he knows a little more, there's no alternative but to keep learning. The only information available to him is inside the residence, so leaving is out of the question. On the other hand, he absolutely must withdraw from the community and think things over. As the residence is large enough and the number of Edenians ever decreasing, Electra J. will not be able to refuse him this favor.

Winston withdrew just when I needed his advice the most, Electra J thinks.

How many times had he told her about the weight of trust placed on the few homeless and sedentary people who lived with him? Now it was Electra J.'s responsibility, and she understands Winston's discomfort better.

The situation between Edenian men and women is still very unstable. The slightest thing can rekindle resentment and destroy the little equilibrium that has timidly returned to the community. To avoid any relapse, Electra J. has decided to continue the capsule rations of Jouvence while stocks last.

"Electra J. decided this, Electra J. checked that." No sooner had she returned than she was in charge. She can't help but think of her father and the countless decisions he made every day, some of which Electra J. has never forgiven him for. She feels she's becoming just like him, inexorably, a curse she can't escape, and which horrifies her.

Another decision can't wait to be made: what to do with the rest of Winston's community, still at the Weert rehabilitation center since they left for the Brussels Megalopolis via the metro tunnels?

She remembers what Nucleus used to say. "If we are to have any chance of completing this renaissance, we must be able to sacrifice everything that is not Edenian. Without a drastic policy, we will inevitably fail."

At the time, her father didn't get the big picture she sees now, but Electra J. is convinced that even today, despite the infertility of Edenians and the planet's spectacular depopulation, he wouldn't have changed his mind.

But she sees things differently. There are women there who can carry their embryos to term. Some come from the streets; they've overcome viruses and pollution, and their bodies are resilient. Chances are they'll be able to conceive and give hope to a population in dire need of it. In any case, there aren't many alternatives. If the Edenians have to disappear, at least she'll have tried everything.

Tomorrow, she will speak before the Ecclesia. She'll tell her story to the assembly of Edenians and convince them.

It has to be.

When the expedition returns from the rehabilitation center, the whole residence is ready to welcome the survivors as true martyrs whose suffering will save the Edenians from their sins. Winston, on the other hand, knows nothing of what's going on. The fact that the vast majority of the population has never been in direct contact with any of the real sedentary people of the Megalopolis, let alone the homeless, is certainly no stranger to this collegiate infatuation. And in times of great distress, such as these, the misfortune of the most unfortunate is reassuring in spite of everything.

The rescuers first discovers some twenty women, barely alive, amid the putrifying remains of the massacres the center has witnessed. Every stage of the expedition is reported to the Eclesia in real time, with live commentary and images. Not a single Edenian family is missing, despite the horror of the details revealed.

"No one knows who carried these abominations - the women remained prostrate, even as we arrived. We found them with vacant stares, eating royal jelly directly from the overturned containers on the floor and wading in their own excrement. Many of them had suffered fractures that prevented any movement. As we continued our investigation to understand what had happened, we found, neatly arranged, the remains of nearly twenty infants. A bit further on, we discovered what we believe is the protein generator. It was the others decomposing corpses hanging nearby that made us realize what the main ingredient of royal jelly was."

Electra J. is in tears, terrified that she might recognize some of them. When the rescue team was put together, she had not been authorized by the Edenian assembly to take part in the expedition. Waiting and inaction had been intolerable for her ever since. The hope of finding survivors has quickly given way to the horror upon discovering the mortuary chamber where the infants lay. The pain Electra feels is as raw as if she has lost all thoses children herself. How can one possibly hold on to hope in the face of this Dantean spectacle?

When the vehicle's doors finally open and the crowd discovers what's inside, fear spreads among Edenians at the speed of consciousness. First of all, for those closest to the scene, an appalling odor, a mixture of onion stench, fecal matter and flesh-impregnated filth, infect the air they breathe to the point where they instinctively recoil.

The women, more dead than alive, inertly offer their cadaverous nudity and infirmities, waiting for a kind soul to carry them out of the vehicle, but no one can bring themselves to do so. So there they remain, like desiccated puppets soaked in a septic tank. The rescuers, who had initially equipped themselves with masks to survive the risk of pollution but could have taken them off in the vehicle, left them on the whole way back, so as to be able to bear the proximity of the wretched women's smell. Nor could they bring themselves to describe the real conditions in which they were transporting the unfortunate women.

After hours of cleansing and care, provided by a few unlucky Edenians chosen at random who had probably never imagined that they would one day have to undergo such torture, the poor souls, still unconscious, are finally presentable on their hospital bed.

A quick medical check-up determined the reasons for their fractures. The homeless people's diet, based exclusively on royal jelly, was enriched with a powerful corticoid treatment designed to weaken the bones of the future supplicants to facilitate the crusher's work essential for the royal jelly recipe. This treatment was intended to last for the few weeks the homeless spent preparing for the sedimentary status exam. After that, the side effects of the molecules were horrendous, and the staggering emptiness in the eyes of the few who were still vaguely conscious left no doubt as to their psychological state. While their bodies may eventually recover from the torments they endured, their spirits are forever lost. The Edenians manage to communicate painfully with one of them, who also ended up in a coma. They understood that the executioners were soldiers from the armies of freedom. They had tortured and killed most of them, and abused the survivors

In the residence, as the months go by, the pregnancies of these unaware for weeks on end. However, one day, they all collapsed at the same time, for no apparent reason.

In the residence, over the months, these unconscious women, initially regarded unanimously as blessed martyrs end up dividing the Edenians. While Some see in them nothing more than the opportunity of a functional womb and therefore demand that the inert yet fertile bodies be inseminated with Edenian seeds, other are outraged by this inhuman prospect.

The Ecclesia is torn apart, and orators take turns speaking on the subject without ever truly convincing a majority or deciding the fate of the women.

Everyone is afraid; afraid of a future without children or afraid of an inhuman decision that would start it all again.

In the end, after carrying out the necessary tests on one of them, it becomes obvious that the inseminations performed with noble seeds would be successful.

All the fertile women with a flat electroencephalogram are therefore inseminated.

Pontederia crassipes seems to have stopped invading, for the lack of new territory to conquer. As far as the eye can see and over 360°, the ground is entirely green. Regularly, myriads of mauve dots decorate the invader, like the impressive collection of military awards that generals of another era liked to cover their uniform jackets with.

Only the residence's dome remains. Endlessly covered over, but still standing, it remains the only bulwark between the Edenians and the Garden of Eden; the thin protection that still allows residents to proclaim themselves the masters of the planet. Unfortunately, the sweet routine that has come to punctuate the lives of the residence's Edenians can only be short-lived.

Intelligence is there, and its accomplice, the brain, calculating, egotistical, without compassion or law, elaborates in the subconscious basements of some Edenians plans for ever greater pleasure. This eternal quest soon becomes an obsession, and this obsession is a terrible source of frustration. Unfortunately, it's at the expense of others that the needs created by these frustrations can be satisfied, since it's in comparison that they manifest themselves. In a society based on power and money, the most frustrated will do everything in their power to obtain more power and money; in a society based on enjoyment and happiness, they will want to enjoy more and be among the happiest. This is a behavioral disease that has affected a very small but constant percentage of the population since the earliest traces of civilization. Unfortunately, it often presents itself under the guise of exceptional qualities: perseverance, skill, finesse, risk-taking, entrepreneurship, intelligence, oratory. It's very easy for the rest of us to fall for it.

Pierre has all these talents.

Today, he's part of a group of ten, randomly selected and tasked with pruning the thick, extremely dense carpet formed by Pontederia crassipes, which makes movement almost impossible and threatens the integrity of the dome. The plant can grow to 300 cm, which is considerable for this species, even if it is genetically modified, and every day, the Edenian assembly, the Ecclesia, draws lots for a certain number of gardeners.

Having long been a chore that everyone wanted to be free of, over time it became an opportunity for many to enjoy the pleasure of the flesh in the wilderness. While the air was now of much better quality, thanks to the plant, the sun was as aggressive as ever, and very few dared to go out on other occasions.

Pierre's entire life was devoted to the Orson family. Initially trained by Nucleus, who had recognized early on in him the skills that forge the best collaborators, he then took part in Christ's lightning rise to power. He had very nearly lost all hope of salvation in the exercise of this function, so sick was this despot. In the end, it was the women who had sworn his doom for assisting these criminals. He had nearly been lynched along with the most virulent Edenians. However, in the end, in view of his insignificant birth condition, he had simply been forgotten in the theater. He is now integrated, by default, into Edenian society, which has other things to worry about than the fate of this sedentary opportunist. He has forgotten nothing of his disappointed hopes, his aborted rise, his hated stock, and he silently rages, galvanized by hatred.

Among those drawn that morning was Constance. Her only constant is her power over men, for adolescence is by nature fickle. At an age to be counted on the fingers of three hands, her "joie de vivre", her ingenuity, her good humor, the beauty of her complexion and the absolute physiological necessity of perpetuating the race had driven many mad. Yet, until now and despite the social pressures around conception, she had always politely thwarted any lecherous assault. She simply wasn't ready to leave childhood behind. This made Pierre drunk with desire. The promiscuity of life at the residence had forbidden him any maneuver of force. Providence had brought them together for this work party, and Pierre saw it as a sign of destiny.

Constance's body was not found until several days later. Pierre had maintained all this time that he had seen her return to the residence when people began to worry about her absence. Initially, the search turned to the interior of the dome. But the Edenians were quick to doubt his word—after all, he was a sedentary man. The teenager's remains were unrecognizable. The plant had already begun to cover the corpse. A few more days and it would have been impossible to find her. This was undoubtedly what Pierre was counting on to conceal his crime: she would simply have disappeared. Constance's skin was smeared with bruises and wounds whose putrid, purplish contours left no doubt as to the violence of the act.

Confronted with his lies, Pierre will not try to deny them.

"She was too beautiful, I wanted her too much," he declares in justification. He then spends the next twelve hours talking non-stop, describing in detail the abominations he witnessed in the service of Nucleus and Christ. No one asked him anything; no one interrupted him.

"I didn't know my Titi-San, I swear, I didn't know! I'm not going to lose you too?" Electra J.'s pleas slide across the white walls of the hospital where Laetitia, her lifelong friend, has been in a coma for several hours. Only the regular beats of the heart monitor, still attesting to the fragile activity of her heart, can be heard.

"As soon as I heard, I came running. It happened so quickly; I could never have imagined… You spoke to me last time about your illness, as if it were a cold that would soon go away, and we immediately talked about something else. Oh, I blame myself! If you only knew how much I blame myself for not coming to see you more often since your break-up with Jérôme. I always had something more important to do, and it was never the right time."

Electra J. cries big tears. Tears of anger and despair. Tears of loneliness and guilt, but Laetitia doesn't move. Her hand is soft and warm, but invariably motionless and lifeless.

Electra J. recovers a little.

"It's a good thing you didn't come to Banet's trial; it was dreadful."

How to judge such a murderer? Eden's judicial system was only theoretical and had been useless until the discovery of this monster.

"Everything was terrifying! What that degenerate did to that young girl, what he told about his years in the service of my father, then my brother. He kept damning documents, he unpacked everything in front of the Heliea; the acting judge probably didn't want to arrest him. They've known about everything since before Eden. They manipulated everything, engineered everything, to inexorably bring about the genocide of the planet's sedentary population, to which we all turned a blind eye. I knew it, and then I fought fiercely against it, but reading those reports, seeing the courtroom in awe, and the systematic way in which their plan was set up and executed definitely made me sick. And I wasn't the only one who was sickened. On several occasions, eyes turned to me. Edenians are scared and outraged. As the trial progressed, many people discovered the scale of the tragedy that had been played out at the expense of humanity and under their careless noses. After feeling deceived, they're starting to feel guilty, and I know they'll soon want to point the finger of guilt at me. It always takes a guilty party to make others innocent. But I'm not afraid of their judgment; I'm the last representative of this crazy family and I'm ready to pay for it if I have to."

Electra J. pauses and the beeping becomes more urgent.

"The last of the family… Mom died… oh, Mom, how you must have suffered!"

The tears continue to roll down Electra J's cheeks, but the spasms of grief are gone, and with them any hope of redemption.

"My father and brother are dead. No one, not even Winston, will ever forgive me for my lies, my birth, let alone the horrors perpetrated by my father that directly affected him. I'm hopelessly alone and as infertile as the earth that supports us for some time to come. Only you, my Titi-San, give any semblance of meaning to my life…" Another silence.

"You see, even on your hospital bed, unconscious, I only talk about myself. I'm the same breed as Nucleus, egocentric as hell."

The spasms return for a brief moment, like reminiscences of a past life where guilt was still important.

Electra J. manages to calm down again.

"I'd rather tell you about the Eden community. On that front, things are looking up. The Edenians are getting organized and I'm beginning to sense a real enthusiasm for the exercise of Atomic Democracy. And old resentments between men and women seem to be subsiding. Since the few new births conceived by the center's surrogate mothers, Edenians have refocused on education and the family unit. The constitution has just been approved by the assembly. The Banet trial will at least have enabled the judicial structure to be put in place."

A new thought darkens Electra J's words.

"You know, I think this is the last time I'll be able to visit you. I feel very clearly that things have changed. People don't look at me the way they used to, ever since the trial, and for reasons that are always different, but all equally wrong,

I'm systematically excluded from all debates and all important decisions. So, I'll stay here with you, okay? In any case, it's by your side that I feel best and where I'm most useful."

Electra J. sits on the edge of the bed and brings her friend's hand to hers for a tender kiss.

"Forgive me Titi-San, forgive me."

Electra J. will sit by her friend's bedside until she is called to appear before the Heliea.

Pierre was found hanged in his prison room. Was it because he had to tell a jury about all the abjections he had witnessed and aided and abetted? Or was it that he couldn't bear the sentence that was already inevitable? Whatever the case, it took a great deal of willpower and perseverance to get him where he wanted to go: all he had to work with were his shoelaces, a table and a chair.

Far beyond Pierre's trial, it's Electra J, the only descendant of the Orson family, who looms large in the dock. She has been ready to answer for the abuses of her brother and her father before him, since the first day she returned from hospital many years ago. Today, more than ever, her will is inflexible.

Exhausted and disgusted by the endless list of Banet revelations on display once again, the second in a long series that will only end with the major legislative reforms, Electra J. rises to begin her closing argument.

"I am guilty. Guilty of being born a Orson, guilty of having been able to enjoy, from birth and to the detriment of the majority, everything our society deprived others of. I'm guilty of having had financial resources of outrageous proportions. Air to breathe and real food. A family and social life outside the four walls of my estate and a real education.

"I am guilty of having the privilege to live my choices and the means to persevere with them without having to worry about working to survive; of living after the Great Purge, when over ninety nine percent of the planet's population perished. The right to oppose my father without risking my life. The right to flee his despotism and return without losing anything, neither my influence nor my privileges. Finally, I'm guilty of not being able to birth descendants to perpetuate the superior race my father believed in so much, yet which is about to disappear. I share this guilt with all you Edenians, the last survivors of the affluent or parents of the affluent of the previous society. Like me, you didn't know what to do with so much power and means, and you lived lavishly and carefree, at least until our fate caught up with us. We've come to understand, alas too late, that the original fault lies not in having gone astray, but in having persisted and let it happen until we got to where we are today.

"Don't get me wrong, I'm in no way excusing Nucleus Orson. He was a tyrannical, capricious, futile, seductive, manipulative man. He was nonetheless paradoxically full of love for his people, for all of us. He was endearing in the insane dream he was able to carry out and hide so well from us, who didn't want to know. But the real question raised by these trials is that of the fairness of citizens before the law. Long before the advent of Eden, the fabricated, shifting, and contradictory proclamations of the cartel leaders—shaped by my father, my brother, their allies, and the powerful figures who came before them—should have been scrutinized through the lens of objective, materially verifiable truth. A fair and independent judicial process would undoubtedly have demonstrated the absurdities of the positions taken. We should have taken our destiny into our own hands, and unfortunately, we've come to understand too late just how dangerous it is to entrust our lives to megalomaniacs. It wasn't written, it didn't need to happen. We tacitly accepted the ravings of Nucleus when they were presented to us by the leaders of the governments that worked at his bidding. And so, from small exactions to big lies, we have mixed sordid reality with the most outrageous fantasies. We have gone from a sad but banal affair of corruption and power to this horrible holocaust that scorns the very essence of our ultimate fight for the survival of the species. Generations of corrupt, perverted and misguided rulers, stealthily abusing the weakest, are in the dock.

"Edenians, when a society moves away from or frees itself from its founding human principles, the door is wide open to all kinds of abuse because it becomes inhuman and totalitarian.

"I stand in front of this tribunal, ashamed and repentant, ready to incur exemplary sanctions, to answer for all these charges. But I don't accept to answer in front of you, who are at least as guilty as I am. No, the only one I wish to appear before is Winston. He is probably one of the last sedentary people since Pierre's death. He is one of the last representatives of the classes considered inferior, of those who had to work and who, since the disappearance of the tribal social organization of the first ages, suffer the wrath of the most powerful. Winston has known it all, endured it all, overcome it all, and today lives in seclusion somewhere on the bangs of the residence. It is to him that I entrust my confession so that his suffering and that of his fellow men may never be forgotten or excused. My father indirectly killed over ten billion human beings, making him the greatest criminal of all time. However, we, and all those who have enjoyed power before us, have deprived an even greater number of those left behind and sacrificed. I'm going to leave the residence, banished and penitent, in the hope that, before I lose my life, I'll come across some elements that might lead me to believe that all is not lost.

I ask you as a last favor to place everywhere they can be seen, portraits of Winston, portraits of the one who embodies our guilt."

The audience remained silent long after Electra J. had left the courtroom. However, at no point was there any mention of the twenty children removed in the name of segregated racial interests, or of the twenty martyred women of the Weert rehabilitation center.

Decidedly, some deaths are more important than others.

2090

On the day she was ostracized, no one was waiting for Electra J. at the dome gates. She wasn't allowed a vehicle, since she'd been banished with no way of returning. They might as well have executed her on the spot.

None of those cowards had the guts to do it, she thinks, somewhere between disgust and compassion. Thinking twice, she probably wouldn't have had any more guts than anyone else. *On the other hand,* she thought, *perhaps I would have tried to put up some kind of defense... No,* she changed her mind, *my situation is indefensible!*

All in all, Electra J. has a machete, flashlight, dehydrated food and water for three days. This is already a considerable weight. The first few hours of the long walk ahead will be worthy of the Chinese torments recounted in the history books of the Edenians. She will have to die of thirst as she hears the ten liters of thirst-quenching liquid splashing around inside her backpack.

Of all her wardrobe, Electra J. chose to wear the electric blue dress her father had bought her, which she had been very careful never to wear. Why this dress rather than any other? No doubt also because this blue clashes terribly with the green and purple of the Pontederia crassipes as far as the eye can see, and the gray of the sky with no marine reflection.

Maybe he'll be able to see it more easily, she refuses to say.

Electra J. still has hope that Winston will be able to spot her, reach her, save her... It's ridiculous, but her survival instinct is matched only by her stubbornness. But she still doesn't dare take the first step that will initiate her exile. It's too final; there may yet be an alternative to this non-life that awaits her beyond these glass ramparts.

"I can't see them, but I'm sure they're watching me. It's not every day you send a member of the Orson family to the slaughterhouse." Electra J. scans the immediate horizon of the residence one last time with a hard stare that would have reminded her of her father, had she been able to catch herself at the turn of a mirror. Rage pushes her feet into the unknown, and she has to follow them. As she approaches, the dome half-opens and a breath of pure air saturated with overheated oxygen burns her lungs as it did the day she was born.

It's not the first time she's faced the plant with a machete; Edenians regularly went out to prune the plant invader and clear the dome of her empire, but they confined themselves to its strict periphery and no one had ever ventured beyond it. Challenging Pontederia crassipes in its element soon seemed an insurmountable challenge. The plant architecture is astonishingly intertwined, made up of multiple intertwining branches, and like the battle against the mythological hydra, you have to strike relentlessly and with all your might to advance a few unfortunate centimeters. On several occasions, on the verge of exhaustion, Electra has to interrupt the battle to catch her breath and deplete her water supply. Fortunately, the plant's foliage protects her from the sun's merciless rays. As daylight begins to fall, it's almost pleasant to contemplate the scar literally carved out of the branches with a machete. At the end of which Electra J. can still see a small part of the residence's dome.

By going straight ahead, I can always estimate the direction I'm taking. I'm less likely to get lost or go round in circles.

Electra J. has managed the extraordinary feat of not scratching herself too much. She knows all about the effects of Pontederia crassipes secretions and can't afford to make the slightest mistake in this area. With these slightly more positive thoughts, and in a state of exhaustion she had never experienced before, Electra J. fell asleep under the stars. Lulled by the rustle of the wind in the foliage, she imagines, between dream and reality, a utopian future where she will be saved, where the planet will be saved, where her loved ones will be resurrected to share her happiness.

When she wakes up, the branches are still swaying in a relatively cool breeze compared with the previous day, and the ground, protected by the greenery, is relatively cool too. On the other hand, the scar so severely cut into the plant structure has completely disappeared. Electra J. is surrounded by green. She can still see the top of the dome, but not much more.

A shiver runs down her back like a cockroach along a baseboard (there are always many). One more day and the dome will be gone if she continues at this pace but, with it, will disappear any possibility of finding her way in this vegetable hell.

The days and nights went by like clockwork in Electra J.'s unequal battle against omens, fate and the plant's passive aggression. The caution she had exercised to avoid the bite of Pontederia crassipes has gradually faded, in proportion to the lapping sound that tortured her from inside her backpack on the first day of her banishment. Water is running out, and the self-imposed rationing is wearing her down even further, slowing her down considerably. The wounds inflicted by the plant make her weaker and weaker, and this fatigue makes her more likely to cut herself on the branches.

After six days of relentless struggle, Electra J. is completely lost, has run out of provisions and water, and doesn't even know which way to hit the plant to move forward. Maybe she's going round in circles a few hundred meters from the dome. Perhaps the Edenians are spying on her from the heights of the theater, laughing at her vain perseverance. Electra J. drops her machete and throws her bag in what she imagines to be the direction of the dome, trying to release an expletive of despair that gets stuck in her parched throat.

"I can't take it anymore;" she finally admits to herself. "Even if I knew where I was going, I don't even know where I have to go to get out of this."

If there had been a single drop of fluid left in her body, Electra J. would have offered it up in tears. She remains in this limbo between consciousness and coma, where despair is stronger than her instinct for self-preservation, until nightfall. In the cool of the night, Electra J. regains a few moments of lucidity, allowing her to think even though her body still stubbornly refuses to move. She recalls the nightmare she'd lived through underground, crawling between the plant's roots, and remembers their strange flavors. She revels in imagining herself feasting on the generous sap, at once thirst-quenching, nourishing and hallucinogenic. Just what she needs at this moment.

As if suddenly possessed by a demon, Electra J. grabs the machete and turns to face the Pontederia crassipes. She tears off what's left of the skin on her knees, if that's still possible, and stabs her enemy where one of the trunks sinks into the ground. Her strength is that of despair, she can barely see, and her body suffers so many abrasions that she can't feel a thing. She has exchanged her brief moment of consciousness for a few minutes of pure strength, and, without respite, she strikes the ground around the green monster's foot. The ground is soft under the foliage and yields easily to the human beast's assaults. She knows instinctively that she must dig as deep as she can to avoid the plant's evil properties and take advantage of what the roots have to offer. When she finally recognizes the particular texture of the underground part of the Pontederia crassipes, a slight cut is all it takes to release the raw sap, which spills onto the ground, her face and hands. Without the slightest regard for the centuries of civilization that have shaped her upbringing, the generations of capitalists that have raised her to the highest peaks of human society and in a state of filth and physical desolation that would have filled the humblest homeless man with compassion, she licks greedily at her fingers, her arms, the mud around her so as not to lose any of the providential liquid. Once satiated, Electra J. extricates herself in extremis from the bowl of clay from which she was about to drown, and slumps into its rim in a state bordering on an ethylic coma. The hallucinogenic effects, combined with her disastrous state of dehydration, propel her almost instantly to the brink of delirium.

"Pardon me," she whispers in the ear of her brother, whom she discovers motionless, bathed in a pool of his own blood.

"I'm your big sister and I let you be neglected, humiliated and ridiculed because I didn't want to accept that I hated my father. I'm responsible for what you've become, as much as he is. I knew your suffering, I knew the hiding place under your bed of the little box and I knew the treasures it contained, testimonies to your talent and your frustrations. I'm responsible for your failures because they glorified my successes in the eyes of our father, and I secretly enjoyed them. I'm responsible for your downfall because I preferred to flee rather than face it. You're dead because I didn't know how to use the intelligence Nucleus was so proud of. I'm sorry Christopher, I'm sorry my little brother."

Laetitia approaches the body of Electra J.'s brother and takes her best friend's hand.

"He too died from not being heard? How can you share your doubts and sufferings when those of your friend are so much more important than yours? How can you stop being carefree when your sister's self-centeredness begs for your comfort? I so wish I could hate you, but love and hate can't be commanded, they have to be endured. How can I forget you when there's nowhere else to go? I died as I lived, transparent."

Electra J. lowers her shame-filled eyes to the funeral bed, but it's no longer her brother she finds there, it's her father; Beyond her surprise, seeing him so vulnerable breaks her heart. She remembers all the thoughtfulness he showed her, which she returned a hundredfold. Her adoration for him. At what point did communication become so poor that she didn't realize what was going on and couldn't find the words to make him see reason?

Nucleus suddenly opens his eyes.

"I wanted to offer you the best of all worlds, my darling, free from the wanderings of the past and human mediocrity, but you didn't know how to trust me. You, for whom I literally shaped the destiny of a planet, abandoned me and I lost the will to carry on. All that remained was the putrid scent of the billions of victims who fell under my command, decimated for a cause that no longer made sense in your absence."

Nucleus changes tone.

"Now let them deal with their conflicts, their frustrations, their desires, their needs and you Electra J. deal with it too, you've chosen your side and you're now the mistress of your destiny. If it doesn't live up to your expectations, unfortunately, Dad isn't there to save the day anymore. Maybe there'll be someone else? Will there? No one at all? Frankly, Electra J. I couldn't care less."

All this time, Electra J. remained motionless, petrified by her father's diatribe. She finally turns around in a combative start, eyes closed and both hands over her ears to try and escape this moral torture. But her sudden, irrational gesture propels her directly onto the blade of the knife Winston was holding in his hand, silently, just behind her. Eyes wide with surprise and pain, she holds her breath for what seems like an eternity. Releasing the CO_2 from her lungs, she slumps gently to the ground, held down by Winston.

"You never stopped lying! To your father, to your brother, to your friends, to the survivors of the genocide orchestrated by your kind, and you've never stopped lying to me, out of cowardice, out of complacency, out of necessity; you're no better than your father or any of your kind, and the earth will heal faster without you."

Electra J. had neglected the machete at the bottom of the clay bowl after notching the plant's roots, and the Pontederia crassipes had consolidated the seat of the bladed weapon, blade up, regenerating around it overnight.

Turning around in her delirium, Electra J. had just impaled herself on it. She arches her back one last time in pain. Fate is sometimes singular.

2100:
Extract from the *Pierre de Vent* – Anonymous

After the departure of Electra J. and the discovery of fertile women, everything changed at the residence. Gradually, unbridled sexuality gave way to more intimate, deeper relationships. We discovered the physical plenitude and the serenity that only those who mate regularly and with partners who match them physically and emotionally can know. A bliss that prohibits all parasitic feelings of envy, frustration or aggression. How can you be aggressive when you're fulfilled?

"Despite the precariousness and uncertainties surrounding my future, I am physically fulfilled, according to my needs, in my own way, respecting the desires and needs of the other(s). I know I'm not the only one. We talk about it every day at the assembly. Thanks to these discussions, to the chemical molecules of Jouvence and, above all, to the urgent need to reproduce in order to build a future, all the moralizing locks have come down. They have revealed our true nature and our true needs. In this plenitude, this soothing of body and mind, we have reached the gates of precious happiness: that of enjoying and making others enjoy. To give and receive that most important of pleasures, the one that follows coitus. At this moment, there's no need for control or power. No wealth is great enough to be a substitute, and no warrior's feelings can remain after the explosion of a shared orgasm. Yet nowhere, until now, was it possible to learn the secrets that forge exceptional lovers? No school to guide first experiences? In the past, the carnal relationship, which can neither be apprehended nor transcended without scrupulous, compassionate listening to the other, was reduced to the basic functions of reproduction or masturbatory relief. Worse still, the pornographic images freely disseminated on Big Brother were the illustration of its perfect antithesis. Pornography had succeeded in assimilating sexual relations to terrible jousts where belligerent men and women insult each other, hit each other and adopt warlike expressions borrowed from the most violent battle scenes. It's the ultimate hijacking of the act of love, transforming copulation into an instrument of mass destruction, even before the advent of Jouvence.

Gradually, by dint of debating and trying to find remedies for our ills, we have come to understand the importance of this learning process for the balance of our society. We want to spare our precious few descendants the mistakes of the past.

We have taught our children the elementary rules of human hygiene without shame or restriction. From the earliest age, we have taught them to manage their excrement, to encourage play to stimulate their curiosity and creativity, to learn to appreciate the pleasures of the table and to beware of the dangers of artificial paradises. Finally, at puberty, we have taught them to discover the ecstasy of sexual communion. I'm convinced that these few precepts take precedence over all others and, once acquired, open the door to all the qualities that make a little being into a healthy, balanced adult human being."

"Something has changed," remarks Winston, who spends most of his time reading, observing and meditating away from the hustle and bustle of society.

Over the past few days, the hyacinth's foliage has looked different, which hasn't happened since the plant invasion. The plant looks less fatty, less green and less supple. At first, Winston had been thinking about this in the background without really being aware of it, but as the days go by, the feeling is confirmed. The plant is still lost on the horizon, and no patch of earth is visible, but if it were a person, people would be worried to see how pale it is.

Winston waits a while longer, then decides to come out of retirement to share his observations with Electra J., whose departure he is unaware of.

As he walks through the residence to the theater where the new government is housed, the happy effervescence there takes him by surprise. It literally delights him, even though his somber temperament forbids him to show it, let alone admit it to himself. Everyone's busy, but there's none of the usual bad vibes in the air today. Winston is very sensitive to these pressure variations, caused by everyone's state of mind, which invade the ambient air where people interact. In fact, this was one of the many reasons why he decided to take up hermitage, as these manometric tensions had become unbearable for him. Today, although he feels observed, he perceives no animosity.

Buoyed by his euphoria, he called out to one of the passers-by, thinking that, given his age, the stranger wouldn't dare turn him away too quickly. The Edenian immediately recognized him and greeted him with his biggest smile, which already left Winston rather pensive.

"What a great honor you're doing me here; your absence from the democratic scene was keenly noticed and everyone feared for your health."

Winston had definitely not expected such an introduction and was left dumbfounded.

The Edenian continues, "What can I do for you?"

"Where are you going?" asks Winston, more brutally than he would have liked.

"I'm on my way to the theater to take part in Eden's daily assembly meeting, which most people attend," he adds, smiling wider.

"We also have the opportunity to take part in debates and vote from home, but I have to admit that I particularly appreciate this regular contact with residents. And most of the debates are enriching, and even if everything is done in writing and anonymously, it's always exciting to get together after the debates to continue the conversations and develop our arguments before the next session. The feeling of being able to make a real difference is a little lost when that power is exercised away from the hemicycle. While it's still possible to get everyone together, we've got to make the most of it. When you think that this theater was once our prison, I never imagined I'd have so much fun going back there."

Winston can't believe it.

"How long have these meetings been going on?"

"Since the great trials that followed Banet's conviction, the meetings have never ceased. First, we had to get organized, and when the big assemblies were set up, they immediately legislated—there was so much to do."

Winston changes his plans without really thinking about it.

"Do you think I can attend these meetings?"

The Edenian, for all his respect for Winston, can't help but be amused by his concerns.

"I don't think you'll have any trouble, and the sessions are all open to the public anyway. Here, let me give you this, it will help you better understand why and how we have organized ourselves." The man hands Winston a copy of 'The Practical Guide to Atomic Democracy'.

From room to room, meeting to meeting, Winston is fascinated by what he sees and hears. He experienced a childhood in an isolation room where the other was evil, a pornographic youth where the other was the tool, and an existence where the life of the masses was a negligible quantity. He was finally discovering a new form of society, yet one born of the worst despotic excesses, where the other is essential and benevolent.

Here, citizens draw up laws and there, others vote on them in total silence, since everything is done in writing, connected to the debate software, AGORAPP, designed by Nucleus based on texts by Bouquillard. Elsewhere, citizens are judged for their crimes or disputes by other citizens and according to the same laws.

What Winston discovers, from room to room, goes beyond the wildest utopias. The democratic system, as organized for and by the few thousand individuals remaining at the residence, would undoubtedly have worked even better with a population a hundred thousand times larger. The burden of its operation would have weighed less on the citizens the more numerous they would have been. However, the enthusiasm and conviction of those involved in this new system left no doubt as to its validity and viability.

Unfortunately, Winston also notes that Eden's population is steadily declining, and that this magnificent system will no doubt also be the one that accompanies the species to the grave.

Since his exile, Winston has studied the history of mankind, hoping to fill as much as he can, the abyss of ignorance into which he was plunged during the first part of his life. He relentlessly read the few books that remained at the residence, but above all the countless digitalization that had inadvertently been left online, but which nobody consulted. He discovered the origins of democracy and what our ancestors had done with it. He examined its golden age, its many abolitions, its vain attempts to restore it, and its ultimate perversion in the 18th century, when representative democracies were introduced, culminating in the system in which he grew up. He also read the great philosophers, who led him to question far more existential issues than these social contracts, from the justification of his existence to the essence of his being. His first name: where does it come from? Who gave it to him? Was it a SUB or a sedentary administrator? He's not sure he wants to claim this attribute bestowed by a stranger on a stranger, so many years ago… Winston can't hold back a smile when he thinks of his age. That old fool who finds himself in the middle of a teenage crisis at four times twenty.

At least he knows he can't depart this life without leaving something behind. If he has endured where so many have fallen, then there must be a purpose still waiting for him.

Hours, days and years go by, and Winston searches the books for a clue to help him in his quest. At every turn, he gives thanks to the providence that preserves his eyes to read and his mind to understand. But one day, like all the others, he realizes that the answer to this question is not to be found in books. The digitalization that feeds his quest will disappear the day the instruments that preserve them online cease to function. They still work, he doesn't know how, but just as perpetual motion engines can stop, so can machines that never wear out. With them, the entire history of mankind will disappear. Unlike frescoes in caves or inscriptions carved into granite, virtual data evaporate when centuries jam their cogs, in which case nothing will remain, no trace at all. No faded colors or eroded writing, the virtual is nothing that returns to the nothingness of which it is the illusory shadow. Winston can't stand the idea. While he readily accepts returning to nothingness, he refuses to remain powerless in the face of the dilution of millennial knowledge in digital mists. If mankind was foolish enough to have destroyed all its treasures after digitizing them, it's his duty to return to concreteness what the immateriality of technology has robbed it off of. He is going to transcribe what cannot disappear from human thought.

Slowly, he removes from his pocket the styli that have never left him, stolen during his visit to Nucleus. A light touch of his fingers on the handle and the blade of light begins a long, sub-frequential chorus, the only witness to the activity of the future word sculptor's tool. What could be the support for his enterprise? Is the environment in which he finds himself so perishable that he almost feels pity for such a futile project? Dismissing these doubts with a wave of his head, Winston turns his attention to the immensity of the dome overlooking the residence. The pristine, generous surface and malleable, rot-proof material of this polymethyl methacrylate barrier makes this monument to injustice the perfect herald of an enterprise whose posterity will echo down the centuries! Its first transcription will be the "Practical Guide toward an Atomic Democracy." This political system works. It has appeased the Edenians, the predatory human caste responsible for the planet's ruin. It must endure. As Winston approaches the transparent barrier, he recalls Catherine's memory. It was she who taught him to write, and it's undoubtedly thanks to her that the human experience has a chance of continuing to illuminate the immensity of time. He presses lightly on the handle of the stylus, which obediently begins to vibrate. The first words are uncertain and the letters trembling, but Winston now knows what he was born to do.

Since that day, Winston has stubbornly pursued what has become his sole objective. He copies, as best he can and for as long as he can, what he discovers online, in every language he comes across. Without always knowing what it is, he simply relies on the validity of the choice of the person whom one day decided to put it online. Sometimes his transcription is more like drawing than writing, so foreign is the original language to him, and sometimes what he engraves brings tears to his eyes. He would have liked to be systematic, but the accessibility of the polymethyl methacrylate surface is so random that he had to go with the flow and abandon all the rigor.

He engraves where he can, as he can; sometimes in a horizontal line, sometimes in a column or following the contours of accessible areas, he endlessly engraves the timeless testimonies of intellectuals from the past. His enterprise takes him more regularly into the populated areas of the residence, where the barrier is usable.

The Edenians who dare to venture into his vicinity often spend whole days watching him. They are amazed by his iron will and the immensity of his project, but also stunned by its chaotic execution and convinced of the futility of this superhuman effort. Winston doesn't spare them a glance, his attention locked on the task at hand. He knows it would be pointless to suggest any help whatsoever; if Edenians were the elite of past society, typing has long since supplanted calligraphy in the hierarchy of traditional learning, and nobody knows how to use a stylus anymore.

On certain evenings, however, like the stained glass windows of cathedrals, the rays of the setting sun play with the copyist's engravings, forming a network that disperses the light as if through a prism. The Edenians have become accustomed to knowing the frequency of these evenings. The tradition is to gather at the precise moment when the light bends, creating multiple rainbows that are reflected on all the surfaces of the residence to thunderous applause. Winston has the satisfaction of interacting with members of the community in this way, even if it's in spite of himself.

This day, the tribe of six hundred Edenians at the residence stand outside in awe. No one dares speak for fear of breaking the magic of the moment, for fear of waking up. As far as the eye can see, the Pontederia crassipes has changed color. The edges of the leaves are now brown, and the previously gloriously erect stems have opted for a more humble stance. It's both the planet's new despot that's bending its back, and its regenerating lung that's dangerously weakening. Some rejoice, others fear this new change, but all must realize that a new era is about to begin. The plant has invaded the planet through no fault of its own, and if it decides to leave, the Edenians are just as powerless.

"I'd like to take a sample to study it," says one of the bolder witnesses, whose curiosity is stronger than his fear. "I'd like to understand what weakens the plant so much!"

No one had any authorization to give him, so everyone remained silent. The curious man, who wasn't expecting an answer anyway, takes a few steps forward, breaking the perfect parallel line between the tribe and the green horizon. From his pocket, he took out two small boxes. In one, he placed a leaf and in the other, with infinitely more difficulty in reaching it, a sample of the soil, then returned to the dome, his mind already full of hypotheses.

The eyes of the tribesmen turn to Winston at varying rates. He has once again been designated as the great sage, despite the progress of his mad calligraphic enterprise. No one understands it, and no one has dared to make the slightest comment. To the Edenians' credit, the white beard that modestly hides his broken face, the long gray hair, the weathered complexion and the legend surrounding Winston make him the ideal candidate for the role of patriarch. Legend has it that he's over two hundred years old, but nobody has the guts to go and check with him.

It didn't take long for the apprentice scientist to return to Winston with the results of his rudimentary tests and new certainties.

"The plant is starving. I analyzed the soil sample I'd just taken, and the result was surprising. The Pontederia crassipes had been genetically modified to feed exclusively on the toxic products absorbed by the soil, which had gradually made it unfit for any other crop. Well, it would seem that the plant has done a good job. I couldn't find any of these elements in the sample taken, but I did find countless little living creatures that I didn't know existed. They seem to help the soil to aerate itself and make it porous and fat. The soil is healthy again, and it's undoubtedly this new vigor that's causing the plant to die."

Following the results of these summary analyses, the Edenians are gripped by a kind of madness. For the first time since the death of Nucleus, there is a glimmer of hope in their fateful race toward extinction and oblivion. The earth is purified.

If the earth can heal, then no doubt they can too.

Everyone finds out what is available online, when to sow and how to grow what they call their first crop. In a highly secure area of the residence are the "zero" seeds. These are the seeds that were used to create all the others, used since the Great Purification for the "in vitro" crops that have enabled Eden's inhabitants to survive. When the time comes, the magistrates chosen by lot to protect these precious samples will make them available to the community. No one wants to risk wasting what is probably the last chance to taste real food, and at the same time avoid having to feed on royal jelly reserves when the stock of GMO seeds runs out.

Since it is the hallmark of democracy to consult the people, after many discussions, meetings, legislation and votes, the date for the first seedling has been set for March 10th. This is the ideal time for most vegetables grown from saved seeds.

While no one pays any attention to the months of the year, let alone the seasons, because the climate is the same whatever the time of year under the dome, the Big Brothers have retained the old-fashioned computer custom of displaying the day, month and time in the top right-hand corner of the screen. A boon for all concerned.

Winston steers clear of these new outpourings of happiness. He distrusts hope and enthusiasm almost as much as he distrusts depression and unhappiness. There's no way to protect himself from this feeling, and it's with all guard down that disappointment strikes when the mirages of happiness dissipate and all that's left is chaos. He'll continue to act and feed as he has since his arrival at the residence, waiting to see how things develop.

The day arrives and all these sons and daughters of wealthy dwellers eagerly embark on their apprenticeship as farmers. Before sowing, you have to stir the soil, and without the proper tools, it's much easier to read than to do. Soon, even some of them become so discouraged that they decide to give up trying these organic vegetables if that's the price they have to pay to stop this backbreaking work in the field. Then there's the waiting, the doubting, the fear that the seeds won't grow properly or even one day...

But they're growing, and once again, at harvest time, everyone is back on their feet, and not a single one is missing.

The work is exhausting, and when it's over, many are injured, and all are battered. But in their baskets, they are proud to bring back carrots, zucchinis, watercress, spinach, lettuce, melons, turnips, leeks and radishes from the soil. As agreed at the meetings, everyone resisted the temptation to eat the harvested produce on the spot. Agricultural production is modest, and there's little to waste.

In the evening, the mood is jubilant. Some sing, others dance, and the oldest don't hesitate to open the last bottles of wine and spirits they've been saving in their cellars for a special occasion. Nothing so far has been as special as this evening. While some of the less well-informed break their teeth trying to eat the turnips without cooking them, others, more fortunate, delight in the extraordinary, powerful taste of the carrots, radishes and tomatoes. Everyone treasures the seeds they collect from their mouths or plates, for they are precious.

They have read that these seeds, unlike those available to them at the residence, can be replanted and in turn produce other vegetables. They don't know for sure, of course, but they'd be foolish not to check out what seems to them to be nothing short of a miracle.

2734

I'm old, slow, and tired. I often think back to that night after the first harvest. The helplessness and loneliness that characterize me become unbearable when I reread the last paragraphs engraved on the dome:

"Importuned by the shouts and groans that I associated with joy and celebration; I didn't resolve to come and see until the great silence had once again settled over the residence. A sudden, heavy silence that intrigued me. I was petrified by the pungent, fecal odors that invaded me long before I arrived. All around the Agora, the bodies of Edenians were bathed in their own excrement. Some had choked on their own vomit, their eyes wide with the look of surprise so often associated with the last moments of life. Others died in my arms, beyond my control."

I was totally distraught, and it was only much later that I understood what had happened.

Since the twentieth century, humans had gradually come to associate filth, impurity and disease with all forms of bacteria. To the point where everything had to be aseptic and sterile (a term I've found in many documents of the time, which already foreshadowed our doom). Little by little, the breed became standardized. As the new society enclosed itself in sanitary bubbles, filtering water and air and inundating itself with bactericide, it considerably reduced its capacity to create the antibodies that protected it against microbial life forms. In the 21st century, when the earth also became sterile, the solution adopted was to modify the genetic heritage of foodstuffs so that they could be grown "in vitro" without the risk of contamination. In just a few years, the last natural resistance of the species vanished without anyone really noticing, since sedentary people, like Edenians, lived in their protective cocoons.

Which we did until this first harvest.

The regenerated earth, infested with new bacteria and insects that have developed under the distinguished protection of Pontederia crassipes, has become a violent poison for Edenians. This poison has penetrated cultures and decimated the last representatives of a race on the brink of extinction: Homo sapiens.

Now I'm alone.

Like the Adam of the Bible and the Quran, I wander in my garden with no future.

Life doesn't seem to want to leave me, and I can't bring myself to eliminate the last representative of the race. So I'm going to devote the time I have left to continuing my quest and trying to trace the origin of evil. I continue to read, to transcribe, to accumulate facts in order to understand the process that has led twelve billion people to their doom.

"If Big Brother's calendar is correct, I'm six hundred ninety one years old[x] today and the last child of a race that ruled its planet. The dome is entirely covered with human literature, but I still have so much to transcribe. I'm running out of room here, and I'm going to have to leave this place and pursue it elsewhere."

No one exists who can testify to his past, and his name, which he has carried like a burden since the advent of his erudition, has become unbearable for him. Like the original cellular mitosis, which multiplies as it divides, he decided that Winston would become "Wind Stone."— Pierre de Vent. With this new name, he signs his first opus and will sign all future domes, as long as he has the strength.

The sun is rising on the horizon, and he no longer fears its rays. Has his body become accustomed to it? Has the star of daylight simply lost its power? What used to burn his skin has become a gentle caress, warm and soothing. The air is so full of oxygen it's dizzying to breathe, and the surrounding vegetation is absolutely magnificent. The Pontederia crassipes has certainly worked well. He's made himself a makeshift spear and tomorrow he's off to discover his Eden.

FLASH BACK

NOVEMBER 2080

As far as the eye can see, ash floats in the air, making it unbreathable. Where lush vegetation once made movement almost impossible, all that remains are a few charred trunks, frozen in their desolation.

Mallence has just managed to extricate herself from the rubble of the cellar where she was held prisoner by the UBUNTU warriors. Paradoxically, the enormous pagoda that slumped on top of her seems to have protected her when it probably should have killed her instantly. When she finally managed to dig her way out of the bowels of the skiff, the inert, red-hot bodies of her captors bore witness to the intensity of the nuclear catastrophe that had befallen Africa. She knows that every breath she takes brings her closer to the fatal outcome, but her battered body urges her to breathe. For the first time in her life, she can count every one of her organs, so sensitive and painful have they become.

Her scientific knowledge allows her to determine almost instinctively what is happening to her. Her skin, lips, stomach, gall bladder, pancreas, intestines, breasts, lungs, heart, kidneys and spleen have all been irradiated. If she survived the nuclear explosion, she knows that her organs will gradually shut down. She must hurry back to the laboratory if she is to have any chance of seizing the only alternative open to her.

When everything is razed to the ground, it's easier to get around, and Mallence reaches her old workplace fairly quickly. The wide-open door bears witness to the recent fighting there. Despite her increasingly symptomatic nausea and disorientation, she makes her way to the workroom, trying to ignore, as far as she can, the horror of the martyred bodies littering the white tiled corridors. However, she can't ignore her own reflection in the mirror, which she rushes past before stopping dead in her tracks and taking a few steps backward, cursing what she sees.

Her entire face is covered in lesions caused by the radiation to which she has been exposed. Her beautiful hair is mostly gone as well as her eyebrows. She would have felt sorry for herself if she'd had the chance, instead she resumes her run.

Every second counts, and she knows this carnal envelope is doomed. Her only hope lies in that Homo convertibilis prototype on which she spent her resting hours, hoping it's still where she left it. Even if it is, her laptop will have to be sufficiently recharged to accomplish the task she has set. She will never have the strength or the time to reach the emergency power unit or understand why it didn't trigger automatically. Her calculations and theories, as yet untested on a living subject, would have to prove correct, and the experiment would have to be carried out without incident. Her scientific mind can't accept so many imponderables, but her survival instinct sweeps away all its doubts.

Lost for lost, there's no time to procrastinate. The vault door offers no resistance, and Homo convertibilis has not moved. Her fixed gaze bears witness to the standby mode used in delivery cases to save its autonomy. Mallence's ataxia is becoming increasingly pronounced, and it is with great difficulty and pain that she manages to insert her head into the helmet, which was intended to be tested for years before its first use. Mallence presses "enter" and immediately loses consciousness as the Homo convertibilis comes out of standby mode.

Mallence opens her eyes and sees her inert body next to her. She has no time to mourn the loss of her past shell, as she has only eight hours before she must find a new one and continue her search.

GENESIS:
PREHISTORY OF EDEN

DAWN OF TIME - 2034

Tales and Legends: The Goldsmith[xi]

Please follow this link toward Paul Grignon's work first:
https://www.youtube.com/watch?v=3HdmA3vPbSU

But that's not all.

Goldsmith disliked even the smallest constraints, and the few remaining regulations that limited his insatiable appetite annoyed him terribly. So he managed to make himself indispensable to the candidates for president of the depositors' government, by supporting their election campaigns with money he didn't have. Once a candidate was elected, it didn't matter which one, since he supported them all. He would impose whatever laws suited him on the government. At the risk of losing his financial support if they refused, or of not employing these politicians at the end of their terms.

Very few refused. Financial exchanges were gradually and discreetly deregulated, and the goldsmith took great pleasure and profit from it. And so did the government, since depositors' memories were so short that they were able to enrich themselves with impunity.

They lived happily ever after and had many children. Well, not quite yet, unfortunately, for, despite all their combined efforts, certain individuals among the people persisted in possessing disturbing cognitive abilities. They took the liberty of analyzing and even questioning the Goldsmith's remarkable system. They did so in the name of concepts such as "democracy" and "justice," which the Goldsmith thought he'd gotten rid of forever by usurping the very meaning of these words to describe their exact opposite.

It was at this point that he reached the pinnacle of genius: a salary for life.

The money offered by banks to people to survive, but above all to borrow, enabled lenders to make enough profit, via interest on public or individual loans, not to have to worry about producing any goods or labor. Money multiplied in the accounts of those who controlled it, without even having to worry about market fluctuations.

The "altruist" thus recovered his stake a hundredfold, in colossal international interests, and the mass of lifelong wage earners, the sedentary ones, finally calmed down and praised the grace and goodness of a benevolent system.

Was everyone happy and did they have lots of children? Unfortunately, no, not yet. To achieve the Eden the goldsmith so eagerly awaited, the diversity of the depositors had to be combated at the same time. This led them to live in places as different as the countryside, the city, the islands or the deserts, to speak such different languages and have such different trades, tastes, opinions and cultures.

This had to be made more uniform in order to control them more easily.

Advances in transport and communications technology, and the advent of the Internet were a great help in this respect.

From the computer age onwards, everyone knew what others were doing elsewhere, and more importantly, eventually wanted to do the same.

If this desire didn't come quickly enough, it was shaped by the media through television programs and then through those of the Multimedia Complexes: the "Big Brothers." Controlling information means shaping public opinion as certainly as controlling the creation of money means controlling power at its source. The Brotherhood of Goldsmiths quickly understood this and invested in or took control of the major media (television, newspapers, magazines).

If comfort, modernity and entertainment are undoubtedly the best weapons of propaganda (Roman emperors organized breathtaking games in sumptuous arenas to entertain the people and make them dream), the standardization of religions was the cornerstone of social change.

This meant discrediting the most virulent:

By subsidizing terrorism, and sometimes even creating it out of thin air, if necessary, the real rulers ended up convincing even the most moderate believers that their religion was harmful. Some lost their faith; others chose the one offered to them.

As for fundamentalist terrorists, the world's armies and police forces got rid of them once their murderous mission of destabilizing populations had been accomplished.

In the end, when the only recognized religion was based on a single messiah and a single cross, it didn't take much effort to discredit it and get rid of it.

In the end, the configuration of partner countries had to be reviewed.

By grouping them into larger, more powerful international entities, it was paradoxically easier for the goldsmiths' guild to control them.

There is less risk of slippage when a central government imposes its economy and laws on several vassal countries at the same time. The risks are further reduced when this central government is dependent on superior financial entities, which dictate its conduct according to its needs.

It's hard to argue with those who fund you.

Europe, the United Americas and the Grand Orient were born in the 2040s out of this ultimate necessity.

Once all this had been achieved, all that remained was to implement the social advances and complete the standardization process.

Even the most suspicious could not doubt the intentions of a government whose program was:

- Working at home and company housing were the norm for sedentary workers (the air was far too polluted to allow people to go out on a regular basis anyway).
- Lifetime wages for the entire working population, private and public, guaranteed by the banks.
- Online medicine and justice, free of charge and supported by AI.
- Basic food (royal jelly) and recycled running water in every home.
- Free boarding school education and state pension.
- Reintegration of the homeless in specialized centers.
- The opportunity to earn more and develop new private industries in Africa's new privatized territories.

No one lacked anything, no one complained, except for a few dissidents, outlaws or terrorists discredited by the controlled media.

Who paid for all this?

But nobody paid because money no longer existed! Since the 21st century, it had been replaced by fictitious, dematerialized figures. Banks added these figures to their accounts and those of their depositors, and exchanged them from one account to another and from one bank to another in a closed circuit.

Lifetime wages were interest-free, but loans to governments, and to a lesser extent loans to individuals, were worth their weight in gold, and enabled the big financiers to keep control of everything that was done.

Only then did the goldsmith live happily ever after…

Welcome to a society of great social advances, security and progress.

DEEPEST GRATITUDE

To my beloved Pascale, for believing in me, before I did

To Marie Françoise Epelly and Mélodie Winter, for having the courage to read the first draft of Eden, providing invaluable feedback, and, most importantly, for remaining my friends through it all

To Aziliz Combadière for being an exemplary and stimulating French beta reader and for motivating me to go even further

To Brandy Gibson, whose enthusiasm and support greatly polished the English version of the novel

To Victor Mardikian, who managed to materialize the cover I had been dreaming of

To Rose Mardikian for her thoughtful guidance and help in making the endnotes more polished and professional

To my son Paul, for giving me the motivation to look for original rules in the hope of a fairer world

AN ACKNOWLEDGEMENT
OF THE PROFOUND INFLUENCE THAT SHAPED THE
WRITING OF EDEN

George Orwell, for 1984

Etienne Chouard, for respectfully opening my eyes about democracy

Paul Grignon, for opening my eyes with such intensity through his documentary "Money as Debt", which served as the foundation for the chapter titled "Genesis" that initiated the writing of Eden

Frank Lepage, for turning popular education into a 6-hour sketch over 2 days

Idriss Aberkane, for being a fox amongst the wolves

David Louapre, for his incredible talent as a teacher

Albert Jacquart, for the imperious kindness of his demonstrations.

Aldous Huxley, for Brave New World

Cormac McCarthy, for The Road

Serge Brussolo, for all his amazing short stories

P. D. James, for Children of Men

Ridley Scott, for Blade Runner

Terry Gillian, for Brazil

Taylor Hackford and Andrew Neiderman, for the Devil's Advocate

Richard Fleischer, for Soylent Green

Charlie Chaplin for his unbelievable foresight in The Great Dictator as powerful and relevant today as ever

ENDNOTES

i   Fareed Zakaria, Age of Revolutions (W. W. Norton & Company, 2024)

ii   Microchip Implant (Human). (n.d.). In Wikipedia, The Free Encyclopedia. Retrieved March 27, 2025, from https://en.wikipedia.org/wiki/Microchip_implant_(human)

iii Lyfeblood.com, GCOMradio, & DS Ent. (2015, September 17). Change your channel - Mallence Bart Williams TEDtalks Berlin [Video]. YouTube. https://www.youtube.com/watch?v=AfnruW7yERA

iv Bush, G. W. (2001, September 20). Address to a joint session of Congress and the American people. The White House. https://www.youtube.com/watch?v=l_t8yCldqTc

v ManuPoisson. (2021, November 2). Claude Bourguignon - Proteger les sols pour préserver la biodiversité [Video]. YouTube. https://www.youtube.com/watch?v=K7wbDr_P8NU

vi "Freely inspired by: "Juliette's story" by the Marquis de Sade

vii Rhodes, C. (n.d.). Confession of faith. University of Oregon. Retrieved March 27, 2025, from https://pages.uoregon.edu/kimball/Rhodes-Confession.htm

viii Hyperaccumulator. (n.d.). In Wikipedia, The Free Encyclopedia. Retrieved March 27, 2025, from https://en.wikipedia.org/wiki/Hyperaccumulator
Africanews. (2022, February 26). Congo uses water hyacinth's properties to fight pollution. Africanews. https://www.africanews.com/2022/02/26/congo-uses-water-hyacinth-s-properties-to-fight-pollution//

ix Inspired by « The great dictator » monologue by Charles Chaplin

x Wikipedia contributors. (n.d.). Adam. In Wikipedia, The Free Encyclopedia. Retrieved March 27, 2025, from https://en.wikipedia.org/wiki/Adam

Pascal Bouquillard is a jack-of-all-trades. After graduating from the "Baccalauréat économique et social" in France, he pursued classical music studies at the "École Normale de Musique de Paris", taught for almost 30 years, acted on American stages in South Carolina and published acoustic versions of his favorite songs on the YouTube channel, "pascalsguitar". At the end of the '80s, he spent several years touring Europe and French-speaking countries with the "Trio Français de Guitare", which he co-founded and which specialized in transcriptions of works by early 20th-century composers. Unfortunately, focal dystonia prevents him from pursuing a career as a classical guitarist. He then obtained a scholarship to the "Maitrise de Musique Baroque de Versailles", where he sang as a tenor and was introduced to conducting. In the '90s, he co-founded the progressive rock band Saens, in which he was composer, singer, bassist and acoustic guitarist, and with whom he released three albums: Les Regrets d'Isidore D, Escaping From The Hands Of God and Prophet In A Statistical World. In 1997, he conducted Benjamin Britten's opera "Noah's Ark" at the Cathédrale Saint Louis in Versailles, the Église Saint Augustin in Paris and the Théâtre de Poissy. That same year, he was invited to conduct a group of musicians from the Orchestre National de France at the Théâtre des Champs Élysées, on the occasion of Mstislav Rostropovich's 70th birthday. He then moved to the USA to find the woman he was to marry. Interested by the turn the world economy is taking, he returns to his first political passions.

After more than 5 years of research and reflection as part of a virtual think tank of French citizens, and driven by the anxieties provoked by his discoveries, he launched into the writing of "Eden" and the "Practical Guide toward an Atomic Democracy".

Made in United States
North Haven, CT
01 June 2025

69408760R00153